FLY FISHING FOR TROUT

Dr. Jim Gilford

Illustrations by

Mark Susinno
& Ken Hunter

Phoenix, MD

Distributed exclusively to the book trade by Stackpole Books, 5067 Ritter Road, Mechanicsburg, PA 17055 1-800-732-3669

Cover Painting by
Mark Susinno
Cover Art Compliments of
"Wild Wings Gallery"

PHOTOGRAPHS, DRAWINGS AND CHARTS

Jim Gilford- Pages 6, 7, 30, 42, 43, 50, 51, 52, 54, 55, 56, 58, 59, 60, 62, 63, 70, 71, 72, 74, 76, 78, 79, 80, 81, ASA- 8, 16, 86 Orvis-11, 17 Fenwick-24, 25, 26 Mark Susinno-Cover, 22, 31, 32, 33, 34, 52, 54, 55, 56, 61, 73, 75, 77, 82, 83, 84, 85, 91 Louis Frisno-87, 88, 89 Stren Fishing Line- 38, 39, 40, 41 Ken Hunter -10, 44, 45, 46, 47, 48, 49, 64, 66, 67, 68, 69

Published by FIM Publishing, Inc.
P.O. Box 197, Phoenix, MD 21131

Printed in the United States of America

Pocket Guide to Fishing Series
ISBN 0-917131-00-2

Fly Fishing For Trout
ISBN 0-917131-06-1

FOREWORD

Fly fishing for trout is fun. But for someone just beginning, deciding what tackle to buy and how to use it can be a frustrating experience. If that's your situation, this book is for you. It's written to help you deal with the uncertainties you are sure to encounter at the start and to make learning to catch trout on flies easier and more enjoyable.

All the basic information you will need is in the following chapters. You will learn the basic casts, even though it is recommended you take some lessons from a knowledgeable instructor. Knots, basic entomology, and the other necessary information to catch fish is included. But, unlike just about any other work on the subject, the principal goal of this book is to enable you to put into practice what you have learned before you ever go fishing.

For example, most native trout live in flowing water. By its very nature, flowing water reacts to the terrain below the waterline in a predictable manner. Your problem is that normally you can't see what's below the waterline and must depend on hints the surface water gives you. This is called "reading the water," and is a crucial skill you must acquire if you plan on being successful. You will develop this ability through a unique visual learning approach.

The most important chapter in this book is entitled "Putting It All Together." Here you will be presented with visual stream scenes and scenario situations that will allow you to not only practice making the necessary decisions on how and where to fish a real body of water, but compare your answers with the solutions of the author.

So, good luck. You are entering a new world. A world that will give you enjoyment for the rest of your life. A continuing learning experience on the wonders of some of our more outstanding natural resources.

CONTENTS

6

1 GEARING UP

Basic tackle used in fly fishing for trout includes a rod, reel, fly line and backing, leader and tippet material, and an assortment of flies. A few accessories are also useful, some of which you can get along without but having them handy is a real convenience.

You will be confronted with a large selection of modern fly fishing tackle from which to choose, ranging widely in price and craftsmanship. Understand that no one particular outfit will be ideally suited to all conditions and situations you are likely to encounter in fishing for trout. So as a starting place, decide where you are most likely to fish for trout, in small streams, larger rivers, or stillwater, and select tackle suitable for that type of water. Also recognize the price of the tackle does not always assure quality or performance.

THE FLY REEL

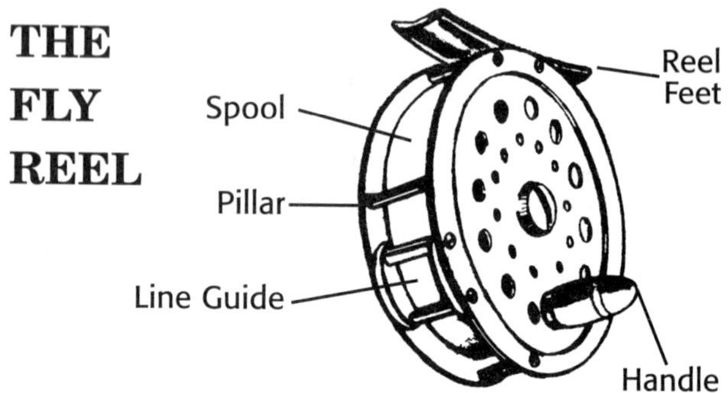

The reel has two functions: to store the portion of the fly line not in use and to take up and give out line as the need arises when fighting a large fish. A reel suitable for trout fishing should be sturdy and assembled with threaded bolts so it can be taken apart to clean or to replace worn or damaged parts.

At a minimum, the reel spool should have capacity to hold an entire fly line. If you intend to fish streams in which you are likely to encounter very large trout, the reel spool should also be able to hold at least 50 yards of backing.

It should have a click-pawl or simple brake-shoe mechanism to prevent the spool from revolving faster than line is being pulled from the reel. Line not pulled away from the reel housing as fast as the revolving spool brings it to the front of the reel is carried back into the housing and may tangle, creating an overrun, jamming the spool.

Three types of fly reels are available: single action, multiplying and automatic; each has advantages and disadvantages. Of the three, the automatic reel is the one least suited for fly fishing. Automatic reels are sturdy and less expensive, but they are heavier and have less space to hold fly line and backing. They have several operational drawbacks, too, which make them a poor choice for fly fishing.

Multiplying and single action reels have a number of features which make them a better choice. They are lighter, have replaceable spools making it possible to switch lines quickly by changing spools. Some also have an adjustable drag.

The multiplying reel retrieves line faster than a single action reel. It has special gearing which revolves the spool more than one revolution with a single turn of the reel handle while a turn of the handle of a single action reel revolves the spool only one time. Because of the gearing, the multiplying reels are more expensive so, unless there is a specific need for a fast retrieve, the single action reel is the most practical of the three types for trout fishing.

Most single action fly reels have either a click-pawl or an adjustable brake shoe drag system; either system is adequate for most trout fishing situations. Tension can be adjusted over a range of settings with a brake shoe drag. Some single action reels have the outer rim of the spool outside of the reel frame allowing anglers to create their own drag system by palming the outer rim of the spool when playing a fish.

Click-pawl and brake shoe drags are designed to function when line is being pulled from the reel but not when the line is reeled in. The drag system of single action fly reels, as they come from the store, usually is set for right-handed reeling. To change from right-handed to left-handed reeling, the click-pawl drag is easily reversed. Brake shoe drags can be reversed, also, but not as easily.

The reel can be seated on the rod with the reel handle on either the right or the left. If you want to hold the rod in your left hand and reel with your right, the reel handle should be on the right. If you want to hold the rod in your right hand, put the handle on the left side. The choice is yours.

When buying a reel, check to see if the feet of the reel will fit in the reel seat of your rod. Most fly rods and reels made for trout fishing are compatible, but not all, so you need to check that out.

A fly reel which is kept free of sand and grit, cleaned periodically and lubricated as recommended by the maker, can be expected to give a lifetime of service even with heavy use. To protect them when they are not in use, some fly reels come with a case or reel bag. For those that do not, a reel case or bag can be bought separately. A heavy sock also makes a suitable reel bag.

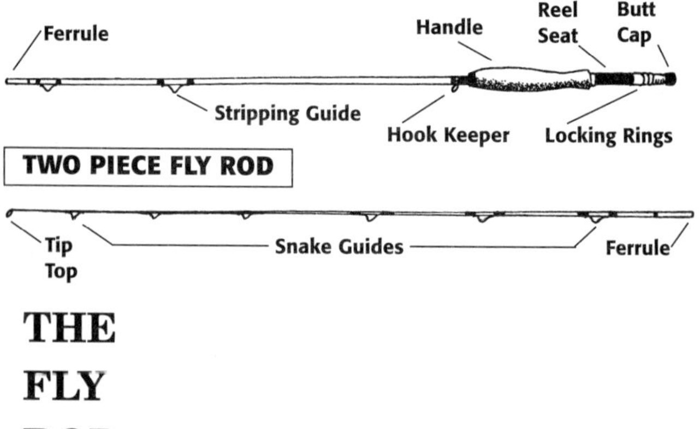

THE FLY ROD

The function of the fly rod is to cast the line. Materials used in making fly rod blanks today include bamboo, fiberglass, graphite and boron. The typical fly rod for trout fishing consists of two sections, a bottom unit called the butt section, which contains the handle and reel seat, and a top unit called the tip section. Some rod makers also produce four or five piece “travel” rods which are easier to carry on a plane or train.

Bamboo rods are solid; the metal ferrule which holds the butt and tip sections together requires some care to keep clean and free of corrosion. Fiberglass, graphite and boron rods are tubular. The ferrule of these rods is created by constructing the entire tip of the butt section, or a post of the same material, so it fits into the butt end of the tip section. Some older fiberglass rods are fitted with metal ferrules.

Attached sequentially along the blank of each section of rod are a number of line guides; their function is hold the line parallel to the rod. The typical trout rod has three types of guides: closest to the handle is a large diameter stripping guide, followed by several snake guides along the blank and a tip top guide at the very tip of the rod. As a rule, excluding the tip top guide, there should be at least one guide for every foot of rod length. They will be spaced closer together nearer the tip of the rod.

The physical features of a rod which affect its performance are: the material from which it is made, its length, and its action. A fourth factor affecting rod performance is the weight of the line being cast. To understand why these features are important when selecting a rod, you need to understand the working relationship between the rod and fly line.

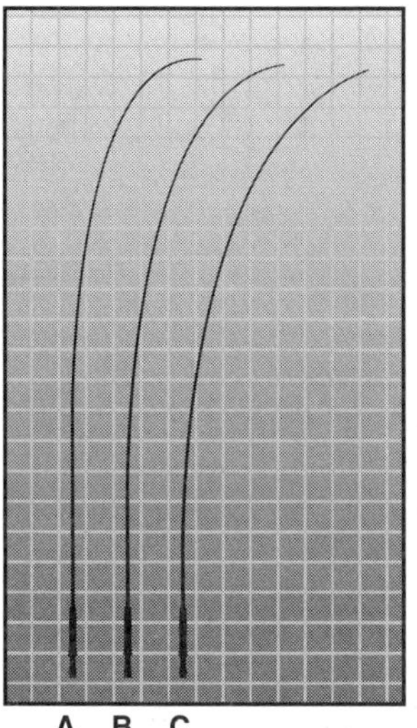

Action refers to the extent of flexing of the rod blank. A fast action rod flexes from the rod tip only a short distance down the blank. At the other extreme, the progressive action rod flexes from the tip to the handle. A fast action rod allows a quick hookset but requires a faster casting stroke to keep time with the flexing (loading and unloading) of the rod tip. Because a progressive action rod takes longer to load and unload, the casting stroke is slower and more relaxed. For that reason, it is the most popular of the rod actions and the best choice for a beginner.

A. Fast Action • B. Medium-Fast Action • C. Progressive Action

A fly line is cast by making a loop form in the line. The loop is shaped like the letter "U" lying on its side. During the cast, the end of the loop at the rod tip is stationary while the free end rolls forward until the loop opens and the line straightens.

The rod acts as a lever to help lift and move the line. Generally, longer rods are more help in lifting and casting. Because of that, longer rods generally are better when long casts, or heavier lines are needed. On small streams, where lighter lines can be used and casting room is limited, extra length can be a disadvantage. Under those conditions, a shorter rod may be preferable.

Fly rods are tapered and flexible. In casting a fly line, the rod flexes during the casting stroke; it bends back as it pulls the line in the direction the cast is to go and then, at the end of the casting stroke, springs forward to form a loop in the line sending it on its way. (The rod is loading when it bends and unloading when it springs forward.)

The amount of loading depends on the weight of the line, the stiffness of the rod and the speed at which the rod moves as it pulls the line. Overshooting of the rod tip as it unloads results in some vibration in the tip which may create waves in the line.

Each material used to make fly rods has properties well-suited to that purpose, as well as some drawbacks. Bamboo has good loading and unloading characteristics. Rods made of it cast well and tip vibrations dampen quickly so it's easier to form a tighter loop and make a smoother cast. But bamboo rods are relatively heavy and expensive and they require more care.

Fiberglass is lighter, less expensive and has fewer design limitations than bamboo. Rods made of fiberglass cast well but they are not as resistant to vibration as bamboo, making it more difficult to cast a smooth line and form a tight loop with a fiberglass rod.

Graphite is lighter than either bamboo or fiberglass. Graphite rods are more expensive than fiberglass, but less expensive than bamboo. Like bamboo, they are relatively resistant to vibrations so they can form a tight loop and cast a smooth line. Boron rods are similar to graphite with respect to weight, resistance to vibrations, and castability but more expensive. Rods made of fiberglass, graphite or boron remain serviceable with much less care than bamboo.

THE LINE, BACKING, LEADER AND TIPPET

In fly casting, the line is cast and the lure is pulled along by the line. How well the line performs that function depends on a number of things: the bulk and weight of the fly, the distance the fly is to be cast, and weight and taper of the line.

Modern fly lines consist of a braided or spun center coated with a layer of vinyl plastic. The vinyl coating also contains UV inhibitors and ingredients which affect buoyancy. Fly lines are about 90 feet long, either uniform in diameter or tapered, and they are made in a variety of weights, densities, and colors, each intended for a particular use. Fly lines are identified by a code which identifies the line taper, weight and density. A popular line used in fishing for trout, for example, is labeled "DT6F." The letters "DT" identify the taper, the number "6" indicates the line weight, and the letter "F" is the line density code.

Fly lines are uniform in diameter or tapered at

one or both ends. Double taper "DT" lines are tapered at both ends, while weight forward "WF" lines are tapered only at the front end. Fly lines without a taper are called level or "L" lines.

The taper aids in casting. The front 30 feet or so of a tapered line, the head, is progressively thinner towards the tip. When the line is cast, a

ABBREVIATIONS FOR DIFFERENT FLY LINES

L – Level (No change in diameter)
DT – Double Tapered
WF – Weight Forward
ST – Shooting Taper
F/S – Floating/Sinking
F – Floating
S – Sinking

loop forms and unrolls. As it rolls towards the tip, each section of line turns over the section ahead of it. As it does, it loses some momentum in overcoming air resistance so it passes on less momentum than it receives.

The taper compensates for the gradual loss of momentum by progressively reducing the weight of the line still to be rolled over. The same loss of momentum occurs with level lines but there is no taper to compensate for it and that is the reason level lines do not cast as well.

The front 25 to 30 feet, the tapered section, of comparable DT and WF lines cast equally well. However, when more than 30 feet of line is to be cast, weight forward lines are better for shooting line while double taper lines are better for making longer roll casts.

Shooting line is done at the end of the casting stroke by releasing extra line, allowing the loop as it unrolls to move farther from the rod tip. As it does, it pulls the extra line with it.

The line behind the head of a weight forward line is light while that behind the head of a double taper line is heavy. A weight forward line is a better shooting line because the line the head has to pull with it is smaller in diameter and lighter than the line the head of a double taper line has to pull.

The double taper line is better for making longer roll casts than a weight forward. The reason is that the light line behind the head of a weight forward line does not have enough mass to force the head to roll over. But the heavy line behind the head of a double taper line has the mass to force the head to roll over.

Variations of the standard WF lines have been designed for specific uses. The head of a bass bug taper is as heavy as the head of a standard weight forward line but shorter. With the weight concentrated in a shorter section of line, the bass bug taper is better suited to rolling over bulky, wind resistant bass flies and popping bugs. Saltwater tapers, similar to the bass bug taper, are made for quick casting to bonefish and tarpon at relatively close range. WF lines, such as the triangle taper, with longer heads offer better control of the line and the fly when the line is on the water.

Line weight codes, which run from 1 to 12, are based on the weight of the first 30 feet of line; the lower the number, the lighter the line. The relationship between code number and line weight is shown in Table A. Heavier lines are used when casting heavier or more wind resistant flies, longer distances or in the wind. Lighter lines are better suited for a more delicate presentation of flies. Table A also shows appropriate uses for specific line weights.

Fly lines are either floaters or sinkers. Some, called sink tip lines, float but a section of the tip sinks. Sinking lines have a designed buoyancy which allows them to suspend just under the surface, or to sink slowly, rapidly or at some rate in between. "F" is the code for floating lines, "I" is for intermediate sinkers, "F/S" for the sink tip lines, and "S," along with some notation of the sink rate, for sinking lines.

No one fly line is ideally suited to all trout fishing situations. Floating lines, either DT or WF,

Table A **WEIGHT TOLERANCE TABLE**

CODE	*WEIGHT	+RANGE	CODE	*WEIGHT	+RANGE
1	60	54-66	7	185	177-193
2	80	74-86	8	210	202-218
3	100	94-106	9	240	230-250
4	120	114-126	10	280	270-290
5	140	134-146	11	330	318-342
6	160	152-168	12	380	368-392

*** = Weight in Grains** **+ = Allowable Tolerances**

are the easiest to lift off the water, the most enjoyable to cast, and the most versatile fly line for trout fishing. They are needed to fish dry flies and terrestrial imitations on the surface. They are also used to fish nymphs, streamers and wet flies under the surface in streams which are relatively shallow.

In deeper streams and ponds, a sink tip or sinking line is needed to put a sinking fly in front of trout which are low in the water column. While sinking lines are the line of choice to take a fly deep, they are much more difficult to lift from the water than a sink tip or floating line.

Because of the surface tension between the water and a sunken line, more effort is needed to lift the line from the water. For that reason, the rod cannot lift as long a section of sunken line before becoming overloaded. Sinking lines are smaller in diameter than floating lines of comparable weight so they encounter less air resistance and can attain greater line speed. Most sinking lines are dark, black, green or brown, colors which are not as easy to see. Because of the combination of speed and hard-to-see colors, sinking lines are not as enjoyable to cast.

As a rule, the color of floating lines are light, white, cream, yellow, chartreuse, for example, rather than dark. There may be some advantage

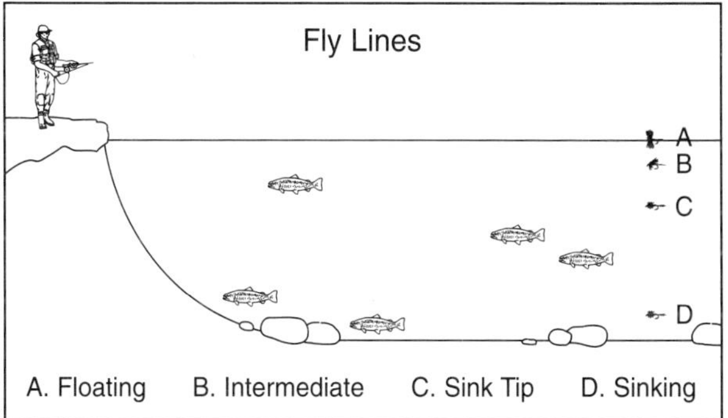

to that arrangement. Trout looking up see a floating line against the sky so a light color is less obvious. On the other hand, trout see a sunken line against a dark background so a dark color is less obvious. Some manufacturers also use unique colors to give their fly lines product recognition.

To complement the functions of the fly line, backing is attached to the back end of the line and a leader to the front end. Backing has two purposes: it serves as an extension of the fly line (which is not needed in most trout fishing situations) and it fills space on the reel spool not needed for storing the line. With backing on the spool, each turn of the reel handle will take in more line, laying it down in larger coils which are less likely to tangle coming off the spool.

Backing should be 15 to 20 pound test, resistant to stretching, and small in diameter. A popular backing which has these properties is braided dacron. Monofilament line is not suitable

FILLING YOUR FLY REEL

Connecting Backing to Fly Line to Leader to Tippet to Fly

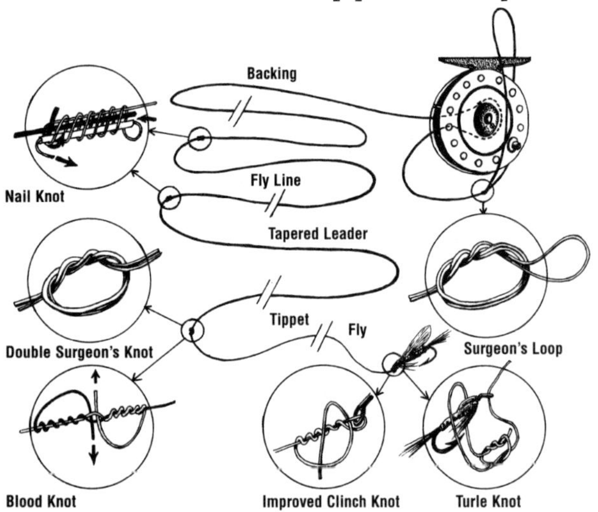

because it stretches if wound on the reel under tension. When the tension is relieved, the stretched line expands, and on occasion may warp or split the spool.

Leaders made of single or braided strands of monofilament are used to connect the fly line to the fly. They may be clear or tinted. Leaders for trout fishing are tapered; they become smaller in diameter going from the butt section, which is tied to the tip of the fly line, to a fine tip or tippet which is light enough to fit through the eye of the hook and place the fly quietly on the water.

The tippet is fine and flexible enough to allow the fly to drift or float freely in a lifelike manner. The taper aids in transmitting momentum from the fly line to the leader. That forces the line to turn over and straighten.

Tapered fly leaders are made in different

lengths with various butt and tippet sizes. To effectively transmit momentum from line to leader, the leader butt should be about 3/4 the diameter of the line at the tip. The length of the leader and the appropriate length and size of the tippet depend on water clarity and the type and size of fly being cast.

Fly leaders of 7 1/2 to 9 ft in length are suitable for most situations and they can be lengthened or shortened by adjusting the length of the tippet if the need arises. Trout are wary normally and they become even more so as water clarity increases. To lessen the chance of scaring trout when the water is low and clear, a longer leader, a finer tippet or a combination of the two is used to increase the distance between the line and the fly and conceal the connection.

Tippet selection is also affected by the size and type of fly being cast. A shorter, heavier tippet is needed to cast bulkier, wind resistant flies which will twist longer, finer tippets. The tippet must also be fine enough to fit through the eye of the fly, yet heavy enough to turn over the fly at the end of the cast. The tippet section of the leader is changed or replaced as the need arises.

Monofilament for tippets is available in several sizes which differ in diameter and strength. It's packaged in spools labeled with a code which reveals the diameter and strength of the material. The code consists of the letter "X" preceded by a number. Table B lists the "X" codes and corresponding diameters and strength. Table B also lists generally compatible sizes of tippets and flies.

Leaders used with sink tip or sinking lines are an exception. To perform well they should be much shorter, a couple of feet at most. Otherwise, while the line will sink the monofilament, which is more buoyant, it will tend to suspend, preventing the line from sinking the fly to the desired depth.

A monofilament leader stored on a reel assumes the shape of the spool and retains the memory so when pulled from the reel, it comes off in coils that should be removed before starting to fish. To remove the memory without damaging the leader, have a fishing partner hold the line near the butt end of the leader while you grasp the leader. With your free hand, run your hand back and forth over the leader to generate frictional heat which destroys the leader's memory. Work backwards from the butt to the tippet until you have worked over the entire leader.

Line Types

Level

Double Taper

Weight Forward

Table B **TIPPET CHOICES (Table of X Codes)**

SIZE	DIAMETER	APPROXIMATE TEST	FLY SIZE
7X	.004	1 lb.	14-25
6X	.005	2 lb.	12-20
5X	.006	3 lb.	10-18
4X	.007	4 lb.	8-16
3X	.008	5 lb.	6-14
2X	.009	6 lb.	4-12
1X	.010	7 lb.	2-10
0X	.011	9 lb.	1-8
8/5	.013	12 lb.	2/0-4

TROUT FLIES

Trout flies include dry flies, wet flies, nymphs and streamers. They either imitate organisms trout eat or something about their shape, color or movement is attractive to a trout. Dry flies are fished on the surface, using a floating line. Wet flies, nymphs and streamers are fished under the surface with either a floating line and sunken leader, or a sink tip or sinking line, depending on the depth and velocity of the water.

Trout flies are made or "tied" of a variety of natural and synthetic materials according to a recipe or pattern. The pattern dictates the specific materials used to tie a particular fly. The end result is a fly that is tied essentially the same way all the time and can be recognized no matter who ties it. Many different dry, wet, nymph and streamer flies are used to catch trout; each has a name and can be identified by its pattern. For example, the pattern for the Royal Coachman, a popular dry fly for trout, is: white wings, brown hackle, red body with a band of peacock herl front and back, and a tail of Golden Pheasant tippets.

Dry flies are used to imitate a variety of adult insects that are found on the water at various times of the year, and eaten by trout. Some of the patterns imitate mayflies which are either emerging or returning to the water to lay eggs. Others imitate emerging or egg laying caddisflies or stoneflies. Still others mimic terrestrial insects such as ants, beetles, grasshoppers and others that are adrift accidentally.

Wet flies and nymphs imitate the larvae of aquatic insects. Depending on how they are manipulated, they can be made to mimic immature larvae on the stream bottom or mature larvae moving to the surface to emerge. Streamers have a fish-like profile and they are manipulated

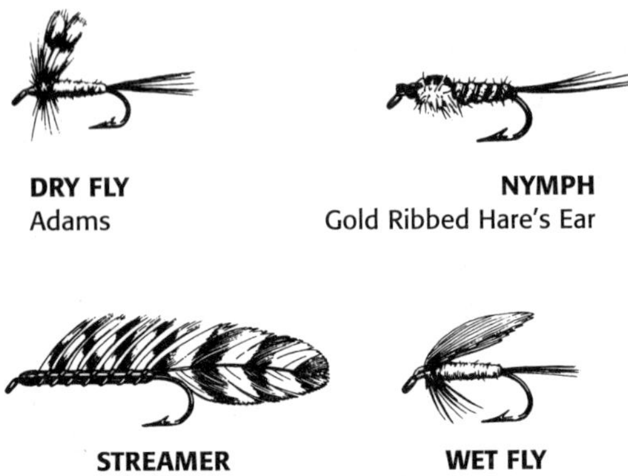

to resemble bait fish which trout prey upon.

The different fly types can be identify by structure as well as appearance. Dry flies are tied on light wire hooks with the wings either in an upright or bent-wing position, and the hackle and tail fibers are stiff. Before use, they are treated with a water repelling floatant. Wet flies, nymphs and streamers are tied on heavier hooks. The body materials usually are absorbent and extra weight is added sometimes to make them sink faster. If present, wings on a wet fly are swept back and the hackle and tail fibers are soft. Nymph and streamer hooks have a longer shank. Nymphs do not have wings although some patterns have one or two pair of wing cases. The wing of a streamer is long and swept back over top of the body to create the minnow-like silhouette.

The same pattern can be tied in different sizes. The size of a fly is expressed as the size of the hook on which it is tied. For example, a #14 fly is tied on a #14 hook. Hook size is based on the distance between the hook point and the shank of the hook immediately above it. Trout flies generally range in size from #24 (small) to #4 (large).

23

OTHER USEFUL GEAR

Other items which you will need or find of use are: a vest, a hat or cap, boots or waders, polaroid sunglasses, landing net, clippers, a pair of hemostats, fly boxes, and floatant for dry flies. You also may want to carry various other items such as a collapsible insect net, rain jacket, strike indicators, an extra reel spool and line, split shot or lead strips, stream thermometer, flashlight and wading staff. These extras are a matter of personal choice based on your own particular needs and desires. You will have to decide for yourself whether the convenience they offer is worth the additional weight and the space they take up in your fly vest.

Fly vests with their many pockets of assorted sizes and tie-on loops make it possible to carry a lot of other paraphernalia that comes in handy on a trout stream. Vests are made for use in fall and winter as well as during spring and summer; those designed with warm weather in mind have a net-like back panel instead of a solid panel. Some of those made for cold weather trout fishing are insulated and are more jacket than vest.

A hat with a wide brim or a cap with a moderate to long bill is a must. It shields your face and eyes from the sun and rain and protects your head from a tailing fly if a forward cast should go bad. The underside of the brim or bill should be a dark color, black or green, to absorb the light reflecting off the water.

Various types of wading gear are worn for trout fishing and again the choice is yours. If you are going to buy only one type, which is how most people start out, you should consider, in addition to quality and price, the depth of the streams, and

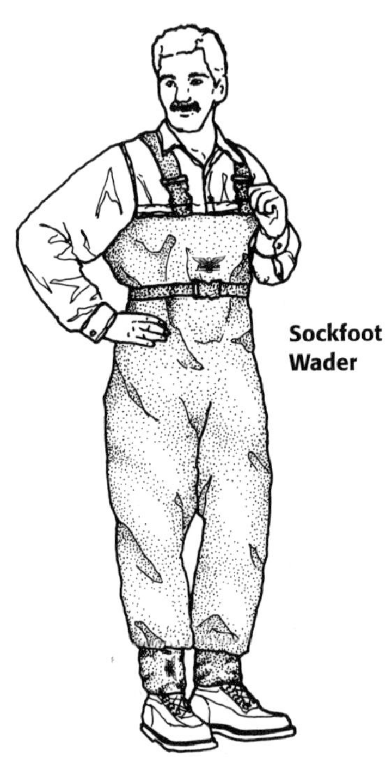

the seasons, in which you are likely to fish.

Types of waders available are hip boots, waist high and chest high waders, with or without insulation, lightweight or heavy weight and with or without felt soles. The hip boots and chest high waders are made with either a bootfoot or a stocking foot; the latter are worn with wading shoes which are purchased separately. Waders are made of rubber, neoprene or a variety of synthetics.

If your trout fishing is likely to be limited to small, relatively shallow streams, hippers will do well, either standard hip boots with felt soles or stockingfoot hippers with wading shoes. But if you intend to fish big water, even part time, chest

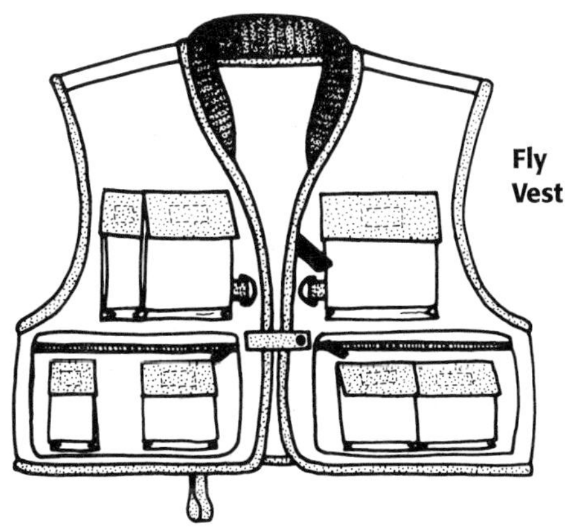

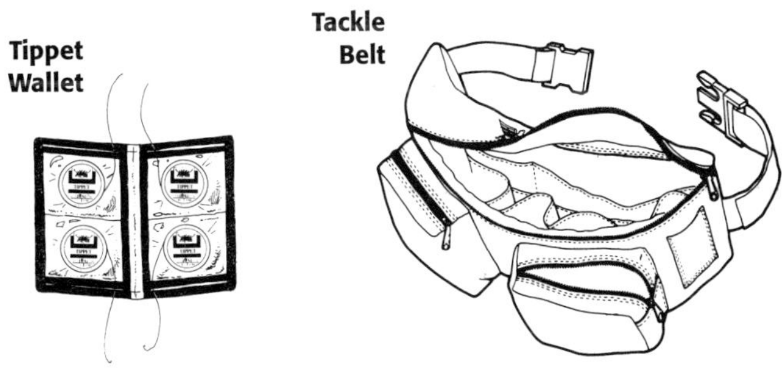

high waders are a better choice. Neoprene waders are snug fitting but not binding. Because they're warm, they are the good choice for early spring, late fall and especially winter wading but they're too warm for comfort in the summer.

Bootfoot waders do not fit as snug so they are much easier to pull on and off. But the extra bulk makes wading more difficult and tiring. Some of the newer lightweight waders, made of state-of-the-art fabrics cool enough for summer wading, when combined with fleece pants and socks are also warm enough for cold weather wading. They are a better choice for beginners who are likely to fish for trout the year around, in small streams as

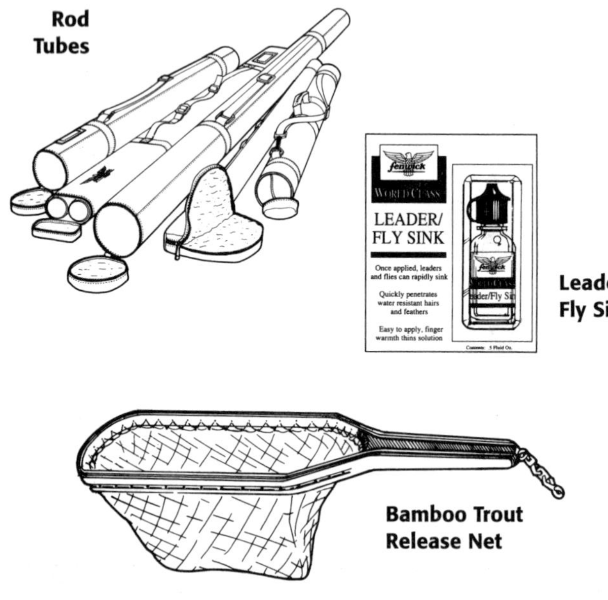

well as large ones.

The foot size of hip boots and bootfoot and stockingfoot waders should be large enough that a pair of heavy wool or fleece socks can be worn with them for warmth. Wading shoes for stocking foot waders should be a size larger than is normally worn in order to accommodate a pair of heavy socks over the wader foot. The socks prevent the fabric of the wader from chafing against the wader shoe.

In addition to the foot size, the inseams of stockingfoot and bootfoot waders must fit properly for comfortable wading. The inseam should be long enough to allow free movement but not so long that the waders will bag or fold at the knees, resulting in chafing and possibly wear on the fabric at that point. When buying waders, try them on; walk around and step up and down to be sure they fit comfortably and allow free movement.

With reasonable care, waders will last many seasons. They should be dried after being used which is easily done by turning them inside out. When not in use, hip boots, waders and wading shoes should be dried and stored in a cool, dry place without folding if possible, preferably hung by the boot or, in the case of stockingfoot waders, by the shoulder straps. Wading gear should be kept away from motors or electric appliances which generate ozone that will deteriorate them.

Polaroid sunglasses are an important aid to wading and to finding fish. They eliminate glare, enabling the wearer to see fish as well as the structure of the stream bottom which would not be possible without them. Polaroids are available in a variety of frames with either plastic or glass-laminated lenses. Care in cleaning and storing polaroid glasses, especially the ones with plastic lenses, is needed to avoid scratching the lenses. Prices vary over a broad range related to the quality of the sunglasses; polaroid lenses also are available as clip-ons for people who wear prescription eyeglasses.

Clippers are used when changing flies or adding a new tippet section to the leader, any time there is a need to cut or trim leader or tippet. Standard drug store variety fingernail clippers are suitable for cutting leader and tippet. More expensive clippers designed especially for this purpose also are available, some of them equipped with a stylet for use in clearing the eye of the hook.

Hemostats have a number of uses, the prime one being the extraction of the fly from a trout. They also are useful in removing a hook from your own skin or clothing, or that of someone else, should the need arise. Hemostats are available in several sizes, with straight or curved tips. The use of longer, curved-tip hemostats makes it easier to see what you are doing.

Fly boxes, sized to fit the pocket of a fly vest

SHOPPING LIST
BASIC EQUIPMENT FOR BEGINNERS

Fly Rod
Fly Reel
Fly Line
Backing
Tapered Leader
Assorted Tippet Material
Assorted Flies
Landing Net
Floatant or Liquid Paste
Fly Box(es)
Fly Vest
Hat or Cap With Bill
Hemostats
Polaroid Sunglasses
Hip Boots or Waders
Clippers

and made of metal or plastic with tight fitting hinged lids, are needed to store and carry flies. Dry fly boxes should be compartmented or have plastic ridges or slots to hold the flies upright and deep enough so the flies are not crushed. Similar boxes, though not as deep, are suitable for holding wet flies, nymphs and streamers.

Floatant, which contains a water repelling ingredient, is put on dry flies to keep them afloat. It may be a liquid, low melting point paste or spray. Fingers are used to dress the fly with liquid and paste type floatants.

Tippet material is made in different diameters ranging from 0X to 8X. It is put up on separate spools suitable for carrying in a fly vest. Sizes most used in trout fishing range from 3X to 8X.

CONVENIENT BUT NOT ESSENTIAL EQUIPMENT

Fly Rod Case
Fly Reel Case
Extra Fly Line
Extra Leaders
Leader Wallet
Tippet Dispenser
Line Cleaner
Assorted Split Shot
Strike Indicators
Nail Knot Tool
Stream Thermometer
Gravel Guards *
Leader Straightener
Flashlight
Flexlight
Rain Jacket or Suit
Wading Staff
Retractor for Clippers
Release Snap for Net
Fingerless Gloves
Wading Belt
Tackle Bag
Fleece Boot Socks

* Keep sand and gravel out of wading shoes

30

2

AQUATIC INSECTS AND THEIR IMITATIONS

Various aquatic insects are part of a trout's daily diet. Mayflies, caddisflies and stoneflies are the most abundant insects found in trout streams and therefore of the greatest interest to trout fishermen. Many of the more effective flies used in fishing for trout are imitations of the larval or adult forms of these three groups of insects.

Aquatic insects spend almost their entire lives underwater. The usual life cycle starts with larval forms which hatch from eggs deposited in the stream. They remain in the stream for about a year, eating and growing. When they are mature, the larval forms emerge from the stream and transform into winged insects which then mate, after which the females return to the stream to lay their eggs. Adult mayflies, caddisflies and stoneflies are short-lived, surviving only a few days as winged insects.

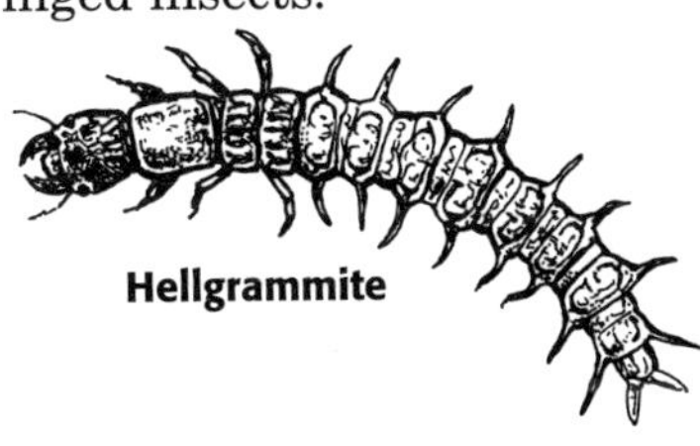
Hellgrammite

With a few exceptions, the life cycle of a particular mayfly from egg to adult lasts a year. The emergence or "hatching" of winged adults is spread out over a week or two about the same time each year. The same stream may have different mayflies, stoneflies and caddisflies emerging concurrently or in sequence. Different hatches may occur throughout the year but most take place from early spring through early summer.

Trout find food by sight. They recognize insects by their size, shape, color and movement. You can do the same to select a fly to imitate an insect which trout are eating. Look closely at one of the insects while holding it in your hand. Then match it as closely as possible with a fly of similar size, color and shape. You do not need to know its name although that would help you select a fly known to be an effective imitator of the insect in your hand.

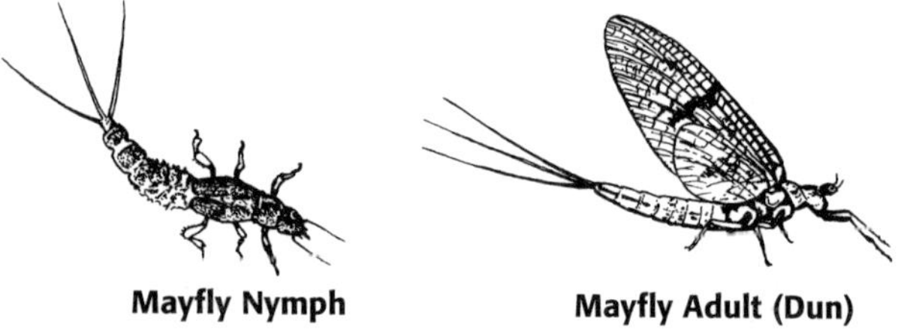

Mayfly Nymph **Mayfly Adult (Dun)**

The aquatic form of mayflies, called nymphs, vary considerably in size, shape and color, but all have the same distinguishing features by which they can be recognized: gills on the sides of the body, two or usually three tails, a single claw at the end of each leg and one pair of visible wing cases. Trout flies known as "nymphs" are used to imitate these juvenile mayflies. Wet flies are used to mimic mayfly nymphs rising to the surface to emerge.

Adult mayflies vary greatly in size and color but they, too, possess an identifying feature: their front wings (some have two pair), which are held upright and together when the mayfly is at rest are shaped like a sail. They have two or three tails and long front legs. Emerging adults, called "duns," have an extra layer of skin covering the body and wings. Before mating, adults molt, after which they are called "spinners." Their wings are clear, except for pigmented areas present in some. When mated females return to the water to lay their eggs, it's called a "spinner fall." Both duns and spinners are imitated by dry flies.

There are two groups of stoneflies; one emerges in the fall and winter, the other in the spring and summer. Adults of the former are very small, black or dark brown, with wings rolled down on the outer edges. Adult spring and summer stoneflies are larger and range in color from black to tan, yellow or green. The identifying characteristics of stonefly nymphs are: two tails, the absence of gills on the sides of the body (gills if present are located in the thorax or chest area, between the legs) and two claws at the end of each leg. The adults have long, relatively narrow bodies. At rest, they fold their wings and hold them flat over their backs.

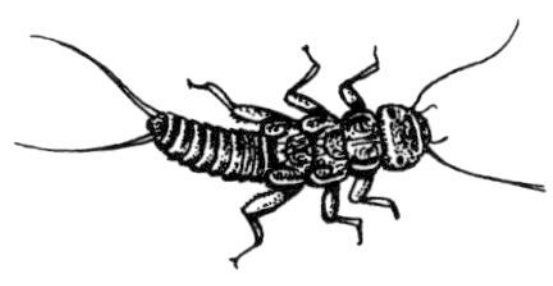

Stonefly Nymph

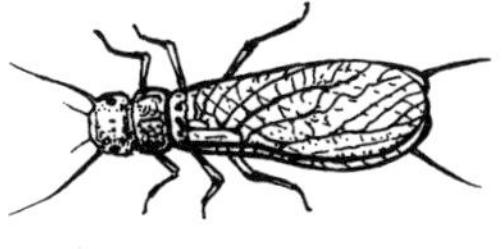

Stonefly Adult

Stonefly life cycles are similar to those of mayflies. Nymphs hatching from eggs laid in the water remain in the stream, eating and growing, for the better part of the year. When the nymphs are mature, they emerge either by rising to the surface where they shed the nymphal skin or by crawling out of the water before breaking out of the nymphal skin. Within days, the winged adults mate and the females return to the stream to lay eggs and die soon after.

Caddisfly adults are moth-like, except their antennae are smooth not hairy, and at rest they hold their two pair of wings folded pup-tent style over their backs. Colors range from black to green, brown or tan; a few are white. Larvae hatching from eggs laid in the water are worm-like. They have a hook at the back of the body which aids in crawling. Some species live in stone, stick or leaf cases of their own making which they pull along with them. Others live in stationary net shelters, also of their own making, and still others move about without a covering.

The caddisfly life cycle differs slightly. The larvae eat and grow for about a year. When they are mature, they withdraw into their cases while

Caddis Larva (Cased)

Caddis Pupa

Caddis Adult

they change their body forms to one adapted for life on land. The transformed larvae, called "pupae," break out of their enclosures and swim to the surface to emerge. Mated females live several days, returning to the water a number of times to lay eggs. Nymph patterns are used to imitate the larvae, wet flies to impersonate the pupae, and dry flies to mimic the adults.

Trout eat other forms of aquatic life including freshwater shrimp, sow bugs, crayfish, damselflies, dragonflies, fishflies and midges. They also feed on a variety of "terrestrial" organisms such as ants, beetles, grasshoppers, bees, bugs of various sorts, leaf hoppers, cicadas and others which fall or are blown into the water. Trout flies, most of them dry flies, are made to imitate terrestrials.

FLIES FOR TROUT

Fly patterns used in fishing for trout number into the thousands. The same pattern may be tied on hooks of different sizes and those fished underwater may be weighted or unweighted. A given pattern may be effective at one time and not another and on some streams but not others. Size and seasonal differences, water conditions, even the time of day and the way the fly is presented may cause trout to take or reject a particular fly.

To cope with these variables, trout fishermen carry an assortment of flies. The make up of the assortment varies from angler to angler. Without a standard to go by, selecting flies that will catch fish under most conditions is difficult for someone just starting to fish for trout. The flies listed below, by name, hook size and fly type, are ones many experienced trout fishermen include in a general trout fly assortment. With experience, other flies will join the beginning assortment and some will be deleted.

GENERAL FLY ASSORTMENT

DRY FLIES

Adams (12-18)
Light Cahill (14-16)
Royal Coachman (12-14)
Brown & White Bivisible (12-14)
Henryville Special (12-16)
Dark Elk Hair Caddis (12-18)
Light Elk Hair Caddis (12-18)
Blue Winger Olive (12-18)
Griffith Gnat (18-24)
Tricos (20-24)

WET FLIES

March Brown (12-14)
Gold Ribbed Hare's Ear (12-16)
Alder (12-14)
Queen of Waters (12-14)
Dark Hendrickson (12-14)
Leadwing Coachman (12-14)
Dark Cahill (12-14)
Black Gnat (14-16)
Blue Dun (12-18)
Blue Quill (14-18)

NYMPHS

Gold Brown Stonefly (4-10)
Ribbed Hare's Ear (10-16)
Muskrat Nymph (12-16)
C.K. Nymph (12-16)
Pheasant Tail (14-16)
Cress Bug (12-14)
Prince Nymph (10-12)
Hex Nymph (4-8)
Fox Squirrel Nymph (10-12)
Shrimp (12-14)

STREAMERS

Woolly Bugger
(Black, Olive) (6-8)
Mickey Finn (6-12)
Black Ghost (6-8)
Little Trout Streamers (6-8)
Muddler Minnow
Black Nose Dace (6-8)
White Marabou Streamer (6-8)
Olive Matuka (6-8)

SOME ADDITIONAL REGIONAL FAVORITES

NORTHEAST

Hendrickson
Red Quill
March Brown
Sulfur
Green Drake
McMurray Ant
Breadcrust
Hewitt Skater
Green Weenie
Deer Hair Inch Worm

SOUTHEAST

Irresistible
Ginger Quill
Mr. Rapidan
Pate Evening Dun
March Brown
Little Black Caddis

MIDWEST

Yellow Drake
Black Quill
Gray Fox
Pale Evening Dun
Red Quill
Gray Drake
Zug Bug
Yellow Marabou Streamer

ROCKIES

Sofa Pillow
Pale Morning Dun
Blue Dun
San Juan Worm
Royal Wulff
Damselfly Nymph
Dark Stonefly Nymph
Montana Nymph
White Zonker Streamer

WEST

Western Green Drake
Gray Drake
Western March Brown
Damselfly Nymph
Green Caddis Nymph
Golden Stonefly

3

KNOTS

Backing, fly line, leader, tippet and fly are joined with knots which when tied properly are as strong as the materials which they join, or almost so. A number of knots can be used for this purpose; three which are particularly suitable are the improved clinch knot, surgeon's knot, and nail knot which are illustrated on the following pages.

The improved clinch knot is used to tie the tippet to the fly. The surgeon's knot is used to join the tippet to the leader. The nail knot is used to tie the backing to the butt end of the fly line and the butt end of the leader to the tip end of the line. The surgeon's knot also is used to tie a loop in the backing from which a slip knot can be formed to attach the backing to the reel.

Properly tied, these knots are dependable. When tying them, the knot should be moistened and tightened by pulling the standing ends of monofilament in opposite directions. Saliva can be used to wet the knot. The knot should be pulled tight with one move; drawing the knot tight by stop-and-go pulling may crush and weaken the monofilament. The tag ends of monofilament should be clipped off as close to the knot as possible.

When tying the tippet to a small fly, some anglers prefer to use a turle knot rather than the improved clinch knot. Whichever of the two is used, the knot may become weakened with use so it should be examined frequently and retied if necessary. A non-slip loop knot may be used to improve the action of large wet flies and streamers.

A system of loop-to-loop connections can be used to join leader to the fly line and to the tippet. A short, heavy section of woven or monofilament with a loop in the free end is attached permanently to the fly line. Similar loops tied in each end of the leader and the butt end of the tippet are used to form loop-to-loop connection between leader and line and leader and tippet as shown. The advantages of this system are speed and ease in changing leader and tippet.

Improved Clinch Knot

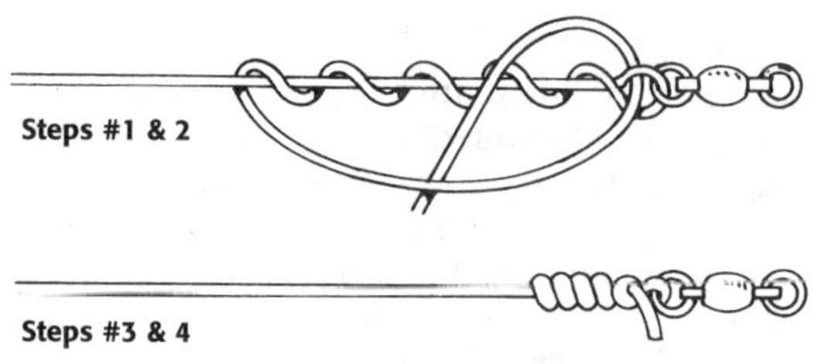

#1 Pass the line through the eye of the hook, swivel, or fly. Double back, and make 5 turns around the standing line.
#2 Holding the coils in place, thread the tag end of the line through the first loop above the eye, then through the big loop.
#3 Hold the tag end and standing line while pulling up the coils. Make sure the coils are in a spiral, not lapping over each other. Slide tight against the eye.
#4 Clip the tag end.

Surgeon's Knot

Step #1

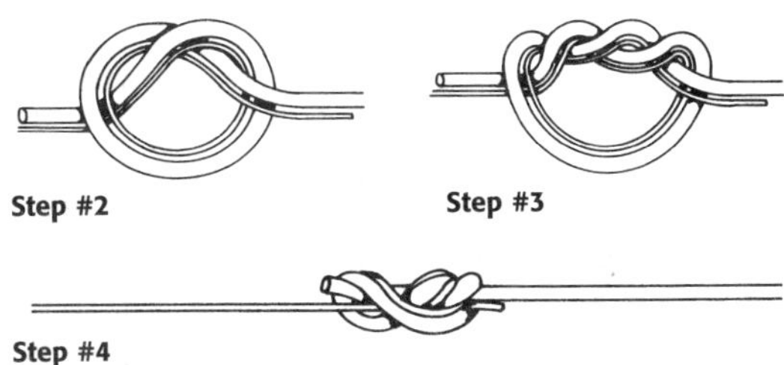

#1 Lay the line and leader alongside each other, overlapping 6-8".
#2 Treating the two like a single line, tie an over-hand knot, pulling the entire leader through the loop.
#3 Leaving the loop of the overhand knot open, pull the tag ends of both the line and leader through again.
#4 Hold both lines and both ends to pull the knot tight. Clip ends close to avoid foul-ups in the rod guides.

Surgeon's Loop

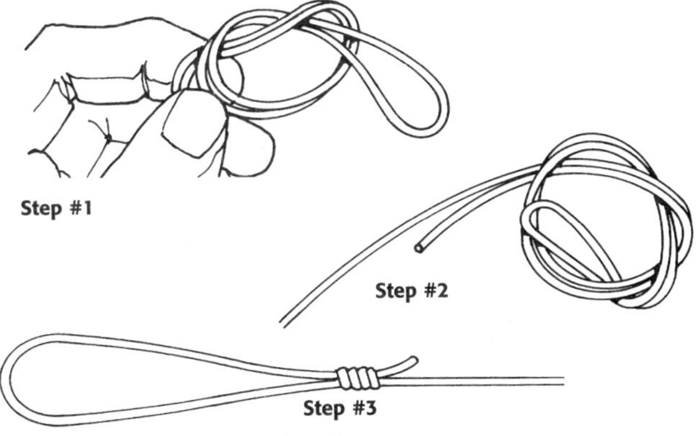

#1 Double the end of the line to form a loop, then tie an overhand knot at the base of the doubled line.

#2 Leaving the loop open, bring the double line through once more.
#3 Hold the standing line and tag end, and pull the loop to tighten the knot. You can adjust the loop size by shifting the loose knot before tightening.
#4 Clip the tag end.

Nail Knot

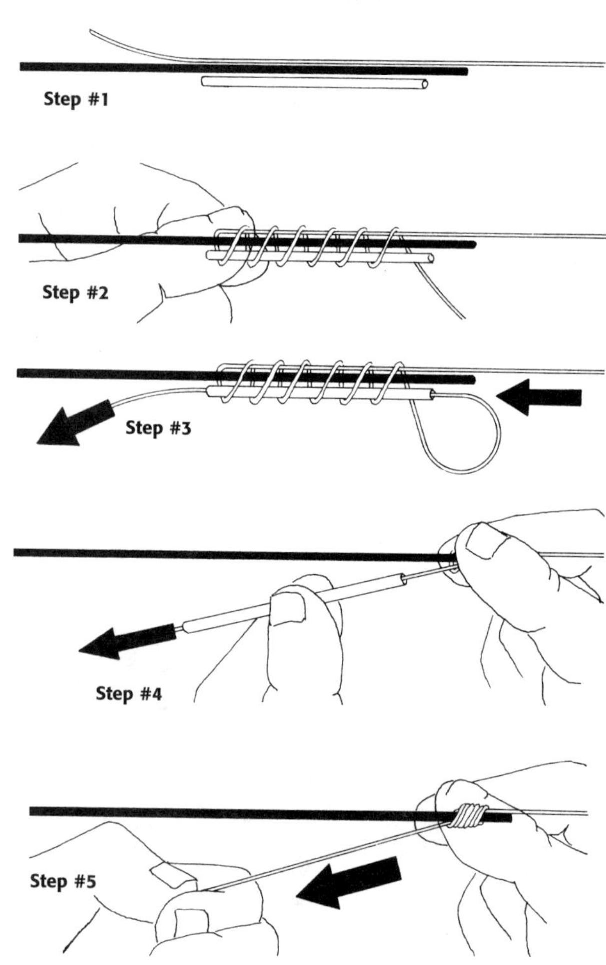

#1 Place tip of fly line and butt end of leader on hollow tube as shown in the diagram.
#2 Hold tube, line and leader between your thumb and first finger. Use your free hand to wrap the tag end of leader butt around tube, fly line and leader as shown.
#3 Make six wraps in clockwise direction. Place each coil tight against previous one (gaps shown are for illustration only). Keep each coil trapped between thumb and first finger. Stop final wrap on top of tube, do not go completely around.
#4 Still keeping the coils trapped between thumb and finger, run butt end of leader through tube, then slide tube from between thumb and finger as shown.
#5 Tighten knot while still between thumb and finger by pulling on both ends of leader. Take up slack gradually by alternating between butt end and free end of leader so front and back coils tighten on line at same time.
#6 Clip tag ends of leader and line close as possible to knot.

Turle Knot

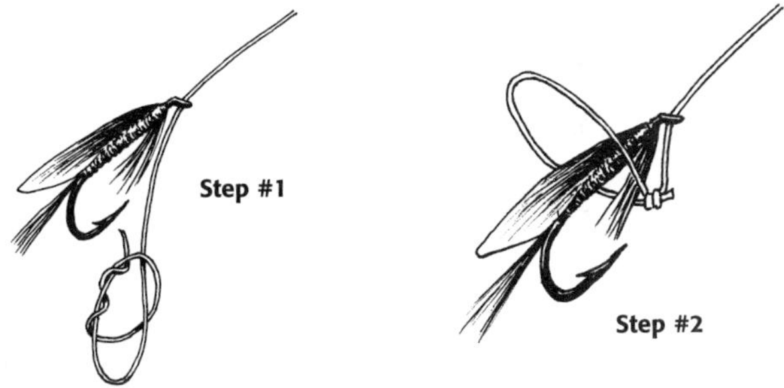

#1 Insert leader through the hook eye and make loop. Tie overhand knot.
#2 Slip loop over fly as shown and draw tight. Cut off tag end.

4

CASTING A FLY ROD AND LANDING A FISH

Fly casting is the means of presenting the fly to the trout. The rod casts the line. The line pulls the leader and fly with it. At the end of the cast, the leader rolls out and places the fly on the water in front of the fish.

Trout fishermen use the overhead cast and the roll cast more than any other and they are the ones that should be mastered first. The overhead cast consists of a backcast followed by a forward

BACKCAST

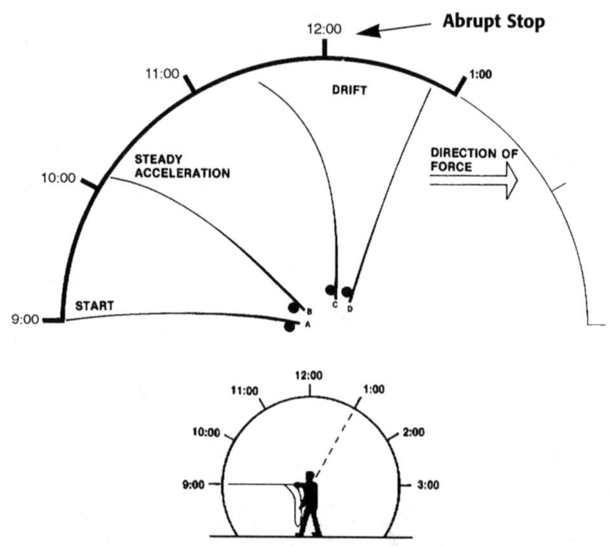

BACKCAST POSITION

cast performed in the following manner:

Imagine there is the face of a large clock to your right. We use the numbers on the face of the clock as a simple way to orient the various positions the rod will occupy when you make a cast. In the 12 o'clock position, the rod would be upright; in the 3 o'clock position the rod would be in the horizontal position, pointing backwards.

1. Start the backcast with the rod at the 9 o'clock position. Take up any slack in the line with your free hand. Note that the rod should be aligned with your forearm.

2. Lift the rod by flexing your elbow and with a smooth, accelerating motion raise the rod to the 12 o'clock position, ABRUPTLY STOP the backward movement. The weight of the line and the

FORWARD CAST

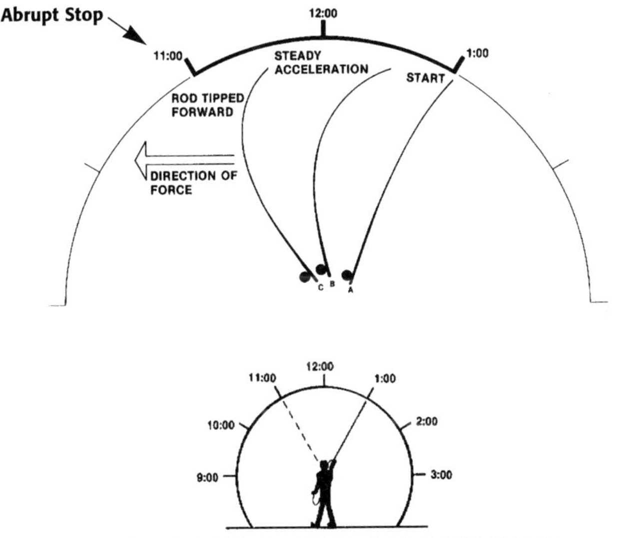

FORWARD CAST POSITION

acceleration combine to bend or load the rod tip. The tip should have a maximum load when the abrupt stop occurs.

3. When the rod stops, the tip unbends or unloads, flipping a loop in the line that carries the line backwards.

4. Just before the line and leader straighten, begin the forward cast. Pull the rod forward by extending your elbow. Start forward slowly, accelerate smoothly. Tilt the rod down and stop abruptly at the 11 o'clock position. The weight of the line and the acceleration load the rod tip. When the rod stops, the tip unloads and flips a loop in the line.

5. When the loop opens and the line straightens, the line will settle on the water. As the line drops, follow it down to the water with the rod tip.

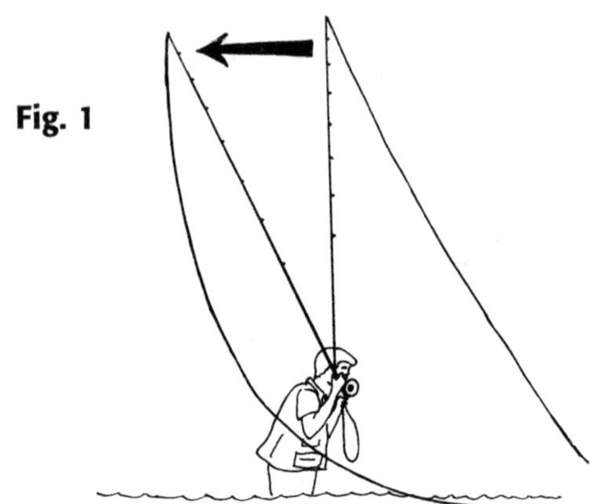
Fig. 1

ROLL CAST

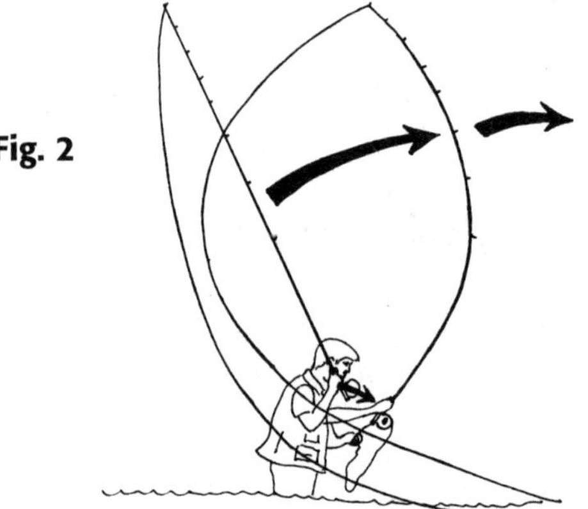
Fig. 2

This cast can be used when there is not enough room behind you for the overhead cast.

Figure #1. To load the rod for a roll cast, raise rod tip, drawing line behind the casting shoulder.

Figure #2. Stop rod in position shown. To begin the roll cast, start smoothly, move rod forward slowly, turn the tip down with a short, accelerated movement and stop abruptly. The rod loads as it pulls the line forward and accelerates. It unloads when stopped forming a loop in the line which then rolls forward in the direction the rod tip is pointing.

CURVE CAST

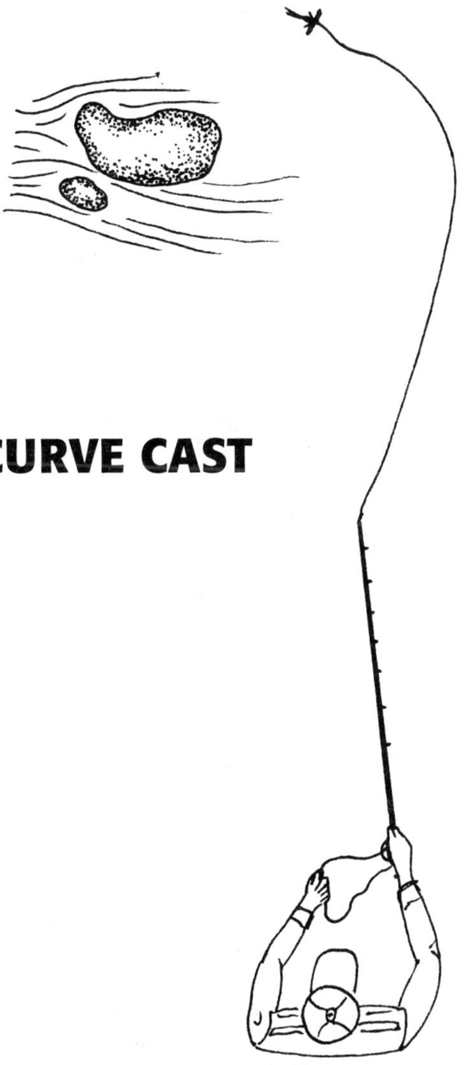

Curve casts can be made by over-powering the forward cast while holding the rod in a horizontal position as shown. Curve casts left are made with forward cast from the right side of body; curve casts right, with forward cast from the left.

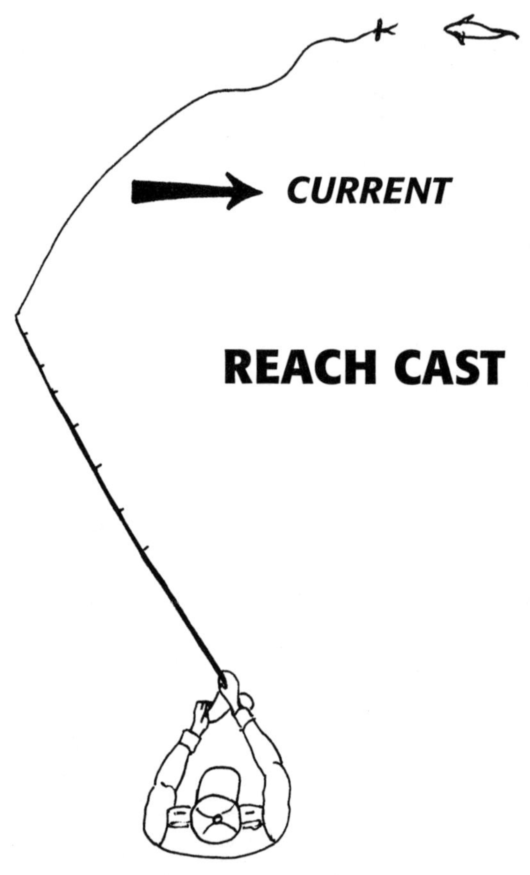

The reach cast is used to keep as much line as possible upstream of a trout's lie in order to drift a fly to it without drag. Make overhead cast which will place the fly several feet ahead of the trout. As soon as the rod is stopped on the forward cast, reach upstream with the rod arm while dropping the rod to a horizontal position. Additional line must be cast to allow for the extra distance covered by the upstream reach.

HOOKING AND LANDING A TROUT

A trout striking a fly moving away from it frequently will hook itself while a short lift of the rod tip is required to hook those which strike a floating or drifting fly.

Playing the fish amounts to giving and retrieving line at the right time. Although not necessary with smaller trout, any loose line should be retrieved. Make the fish fight against the rod by holding up the rod at about a 60° angle so the flex of the tip absorbs the shock of any sudden run. Keep a moderate bend in the rod and let the fish take line if it wants to run and retrieve line when the fish stops. To tire a larger fish, pressure from the side with the rod rather than overhead generally is more effective.

Land fish to be released quickly; handle them as little as possible and use a landing net. When using a net, keep the opening of the net underwater and lead the fish headfirst over or into it. Be prepared for the fish to run when it first sees the net. If barbless hooks are used, it's possible to release a fish without handling it. Run your hand down the leader, grasp the hook and back it out without holding the fish.

Even barbless hooks may be difficult to remove at times. If the fish has taken the fly deep, it might be necessary to cut the tippet, leaving the fly in place. Otherwise, use hemostats to remove flies too difficult to remove by hand. When it's necessary to hold the fish, it is less likely to struggle if you cradle it upside down in your hand.

Fish should be released in a protected area until they regain their strength. Larger fish which may be tired out should be held upright in the water, facing into the current, until they are able to maintain their balance without help. Trout played and released with care will be around to be caught again by you or someone else.

5

READING THE WATER

Not every site in a stream holds trout. Those that do are sheltered from the current. A holding site may serve as a hideaway from predators, a resting place or a feeding station. Although trout may move from one lie to another as stream conditions change, the sites they are most likely to occupy can be located by reading the water.

Reading the water is done by following the path of the current and observing surface turbulence and visualizing what conditions are like beneath the surface to cause it. This is how you locate sites where trout are likely to be found.

Because of frictional resistance, not all of the

Figure #1

water in a stream channel moves at the same speed. That in contact with the bottom and sides of the channel moves slower; the rougher the channel, the greater the frictional resistance. The same is true of water in contact with any obstruction in the channel.

Obstructions and unevenness in a stream channel may be due to ledges, bottom rubble, submerged or partially submerged boulders, tree branches that hang down in the water, fallen trees called sweepers still rooted in the bank, aquatic plants, and various shoreline irregularities. All create turbulence in the water column, producing characteristic surface waves, eddies or whirlpools marking sites sheltered from heavier currents, and providing places for trout to hide, rest or feed in safety.

Water flowing into a boulder in a stream channel piles up against the face of the boulder and is deflected in various directions. If the boulder is submerged, some of the flow is forced upward and over the top, creating a visible hump on the surface a foot or so downstream from the obstruction. Some of it slides down the face of the boulder to circulate in a counterclockwise direction under the surface, forming a vertical eddy of quiet water in front of the boulder from which a trout can watch for food floating downstream, without having to fight the current to stay in place (fig.1 A). If the boulder is only partially submerged, water sweeps around each side and reunites behind it, creating a "quiet spot" on the backside of the boulder (fig. 1 D & E).

The slower current on the outer edges of quieter water behind the boulder is a favorite ambush site and feeding station for trout (fig. 1-3, 1-4). From that position they can see any food item the current carries with it.

Water dropping over the backside of an obstruction may have enough hydraulic force to dig a pool behind it. The heavier the flow coming over the obstruction, the stronger the hydraulic dig and the larger the pool.

Obstructions jutting out from the stream bank create conditions which will attract fish. Water flowing into those obstructions may be deflected away from the bank, creating an eddy behind it. If the current is fast enough, the eddy shows on the surface as a whirlpool. In heavy flows, the fish will tend to hold farther back in the seam between the main current and the eddy currents where it requires less effort on their part to hold their position or intercept food carried in the main flow.

Figure #2

Pocket water contains a conglomerate of fast and slow currents; the surface is smooth in some places but with a turbulence in others that ranges from a choppy surface to standing waves and white water. Pocket water occurs in shallow runs where large rocks and boulders are strewn throughout the channel creating holding water (fig. 2-1 – 2-6); the larger the rocks and boulders, the more turbulence and the more holding water created. Because of its complexity, pocket water has to be read a page at a time, pocket by pocket, boulder by boulder.

Figure #3

In low gradient streams, rooted aquatic vegetation is a common feature, at the edges of the stream as well as in the main channel. Weed growth in the channel, especially in slow flowing meadow streams, limestoners and spring creeks, breaks the flow into a maze of channels. The flow in weedy channels typically is slow and trout take cover at the edge of the weeds to watch from there for food drifting through the channel (fig. 3-1 – 3-5).

Freestone streams are made up of a series of pools connected by riffles, runs or flats. The size

Figure #4

and depth of the pools and the length of the riffles, runs and flats depend on the gradient and vary from one stream reach to another.

Regardless of size, pools consist of a head, middle or basin area, and tail portion (fig. 4 A,B,C). Water enters at the head, flows through the basin and exits the pool at the tail. As the incoming flow enters the pool, it pushes through water already occupying the basin, creating surface turbulence and eddies with upstream circulation on one or both sides of the pool. (fig. 4 D).

Where the gradient for the incoming flow is

steep, the surface turbulence may be strong enough to produce standing waves at the head of the pool. By the time the incoming water reaches the middle of the pool, the current has slowed and the surface turbulence has spread and become greatly reduced. The surface is calm, or nearly so, nearer the tail of the pool where the current picks up as it approaches the outlet to the run beyond.

Pools may be deeper towards the head because of hydraulic digging by the incoming water. The faster the incoming flow and the greater the distance it drops on entering the pool, the deeper the pool will be. The basin becomes shallower towards the tail of the pool.

Various parts of the pool provide hiding places and feeding locations for fish (fig. 4-1 – 4-6). The surface turbulence at the upper end of a pool and deeper water in the basin hide trout from various predators. Trout will station themselves in the slower current next to the seams where the incoming flow pushes past the water already standing in the basin. Those seams are visible so the path the current follows is readable, whether it's in the middle of the pool or shifts to either side. Fish will take up feeding stations near the head of the pool in the eddies on either side of the incoming water (fig. 4-1, 4-5, 4-7); in those locations, they'll be looking towards the tail of the pool as they face into the eddy currents which are moving upstream.

Underneath the area where the surface turbulence begins to spread and diminish, between the head and middle of the pool, there may be a shelf with deeper water behind it. Sheltered from the current, the deep water behind the shelf is another likely resting and feeding station, especially at the extremes in water temperature. Quiet water at the sides and rear of submerged rocks and boulders in the middle and tail sections of the pool (fig. 4-4, 4-6) also provide sheltered feeding stations.

Casting to trout feeding in slow water along stream bank.

The tail of the pool is relatively shallow and at the point where water leaves the pool, the channel narrows. Fish will take up stations close to the outfall, particularly at times when much of their feeding is on the surface or just beneath it (fig. 4-2, 4-3). The outfall lies are used especially in the warmer months when terrestrial insects are active. Although these lies are out of the main current, they are in shallow water and often unprotected except for shadows cast by adjacent trees. But they attract fish because everything which passes through the pool funnels into the outfall.

Water temperature affects activities of trout and the lies in which they are likely to station themselves. In general, much of their lives is spent in feeding and hiding from predators. If insects or other food items are available, trout will feed over a range of temperatures from 40° to 65°. At temperatures outside of this range, they are less likely to feed and more likely to be found in deeper water or, at high temperatures, near sites where turbulence adds oxygen to the water.

Exercise #1

Answers on page 61

5 of the numbered areas above probably hold fish. Check your choices below.

1	4	7	10
2	5	8	11
3	6	9	12

Exercise #2

Answers on page 61

4 of the numbered areas above probably hold fish. Check your choices below.

1	4	7	10
2	5	8	11
3	6	9	12

Exercise 1 Answers: 2, 4, 6, 8, 10

Exercise 2 Answers: 1, 2, 7, 8

6

PRESENTATION

There are three basic requisites for taking trout on a fly: position, fly selection, presentation. Position yourself to cast your fly without alarming the fish. Select a fly of interest to the trout. Present the fly in such a way that the fish believes it's something to eat and takes it. If you see a trout, or suspect by reading the water where one might be, approach the site slowly to avoid alarming the fish as you move into position to cast. To do that and to present your fly so the trout sees it and takes it, you need to be aware of how well the fish can see and consider where it's likely to position itself with respect to the current and the water column under the existing stream conditions.

Although trout react to current in various ways, whether they're hiding, feeding, or resting, they face in the direction of the flow which carries food and oxygen to them. When they're feeding, they station themselves, as a rule, in sites where they can watch for food being carried in the current. These lies or feeding stations usually are located to the side of or beneath the heaviest currents, sheltered in one way or another but close enough to intercept food before it passes. In lakes and ponds with more subtle current except at the inlet and outlet, trout are more likely to cruise in search of food rather than hold in a fixed location.

Trout rely heavily on vision for capturing food and eluding predators. In clear water and with adequate illumination, it is believed they can see objects at distances up to 50 feet or more. Their eyes are capable of focusing independently, and because of the structure of the eyes and their positions in the head, they can focus on objects underwater, near and far, over an 180° field of vision. The forward field of vision of both eyes overlaps, creating in front of the trout a narrow

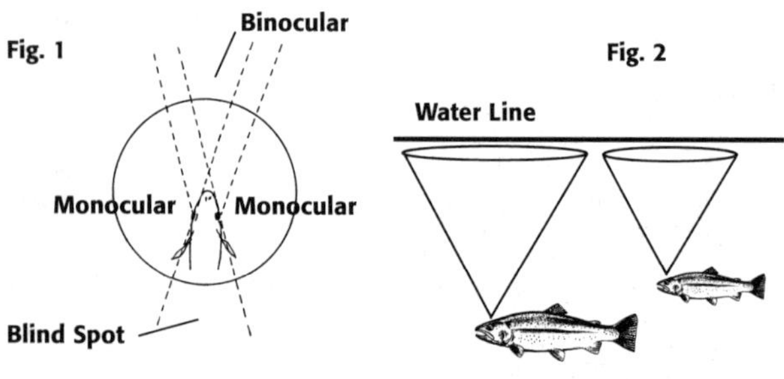

Figure #1– Monocular and binocular vision of a trout. Note the blind spot.
Figure #2– The circular vision window of a trout. The diameter of the cone shaped window depends on the depth at which the trout is located.

area of binocular vision, while in a corresponding angle behind the trout there is a blind spot which lies outside of the field of vision of either eye.

A trout's eyes are not shielded by eyelids and the fish avoid bright light by moving into shaded areas. Given suitable lighting, trout are able to see color, even distinguish between shades of the same color. Flies the same color as the natural food a trout is feeding on are more likely to be accepted.

Because of the structure of their eyes, trout are also able to see objects with very little light. In low light, though, such as exists early and late in the day and on cloudy days, a trout's eyes see objects in black and white rather than color. As a consequence, size and silhouette of a fly are more critical than color in low light conditions.

Because of the way light rays bend on entering and leaving the water, trout see objects on the surface or above the water through a circular window. The window is the top of a cone-shaped field of vision which extends from the eye of the fish to the surface of the water. That cone of vision moves with the trout. The length of the cone and the diameter of the window depends on the depth at which the trout is located; the closer the fish is to the surface, the shorter the cone and the smaller the window.

Trout will place themselves in the best position from which to intercept food, but whether that is high or low in the water column or somewhere in between depends on the abundance and activity of the organisms they are feeding on at the time. Over the period of a year, trout do most of their feeding low in the water column.

Water temperature affects the feeding activities of trout and consequently the lies they occupy at any given time. Rainbow and brown trout are active in water as cold as 45° and as warm as 70° F.; for brook trout, the range is slightly lower. As a rule, except in well oxygenated waters or in

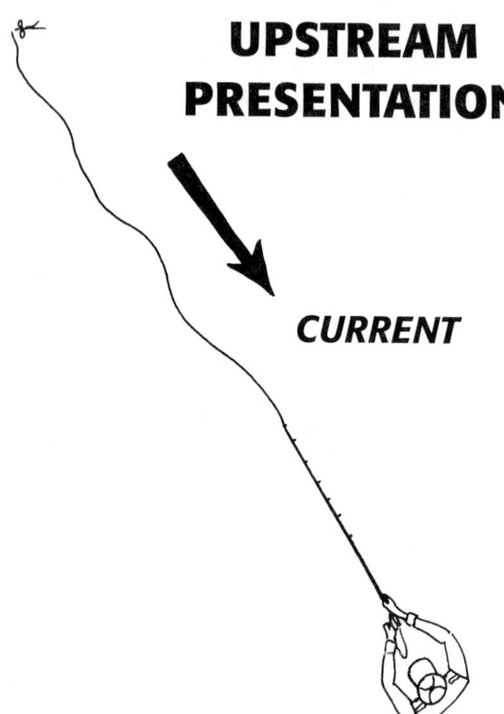

The upstream presentation delivers the fly upstream to rising or feeding fish. The fly is allowed to drift with the current into the trout's feeding window.

the vicinity of a spring hole, trout stop feeding altogether when stream temperatures climb above 72° or fall below 42°.

Stream temperature also affects the availability of insects and other forms of stream life that make up the trout's food chain. Except for midges and fall and winter stoneflies which emerge in water as cold as 40° F. and various terrestrials which become available when stream temperatures are close to the high end of the tolerance range, most insect hatches occur when stream temperatures are between 50° and 70° F.

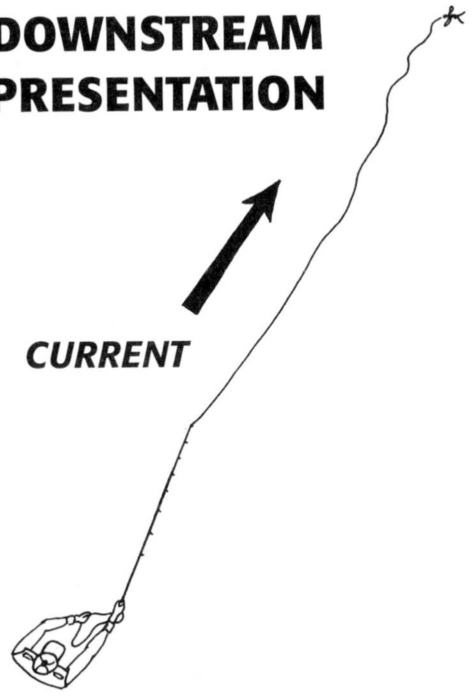

In a downstream presentation, the cast is made downstream. The fly is placed several feet in front of the fish and extra line is released to allow the current to carry the fly downstream to the trout's feeding position.

At times when food appears only sporadically in the drift, trout usually take up a lie on the bottom of the stream and feed whenever the opportunity occurs. But if a hatch is in progress, they will move into active feeding stations which give them ready access to the emerging insects, either midway in the water column or just beneath surface. Their feeding lies are more likely to be close to the surface when terrestrials are on the water or when a spinner fall is in progress.

As a trout moves closer to the surface and the diameter of its window becomes smaller, its view

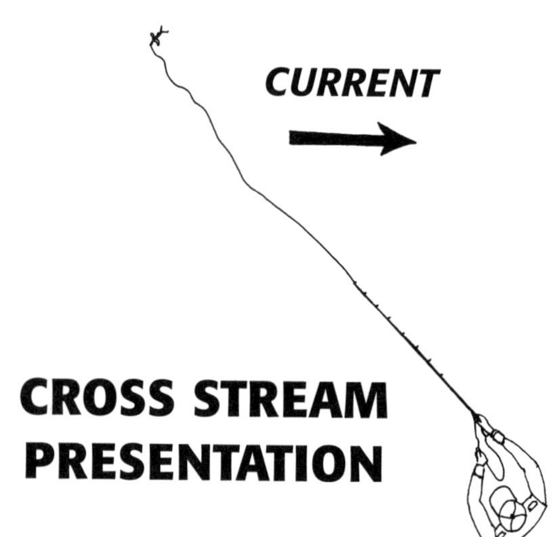

Cross stream presentation is made by casting the fly across and slightly upstream as illustrated. Because the current normally is faster in the middle than at sides of the stream, the line must be mended to prevent drag when using the cross current presentation.

of the outside world also becomes smaller. If it chooses to have a good look at something it's about to eat, it can focus close up on the object.

When a trout is feeding within a few inches of the surface, focusing closely on objects carried to it by the current, its ability to see clearly other objects within its window is reduced. This is the reasons why a trout doesn't see, and therefore doesn't take, a fly that is two or three feet out of its feeding lane. This is also the reason it's possible to move close to trout suspended just below the surface without scaring them.

Fish in the same reach of a stream follow similar activity patterns. For example, in the sum-

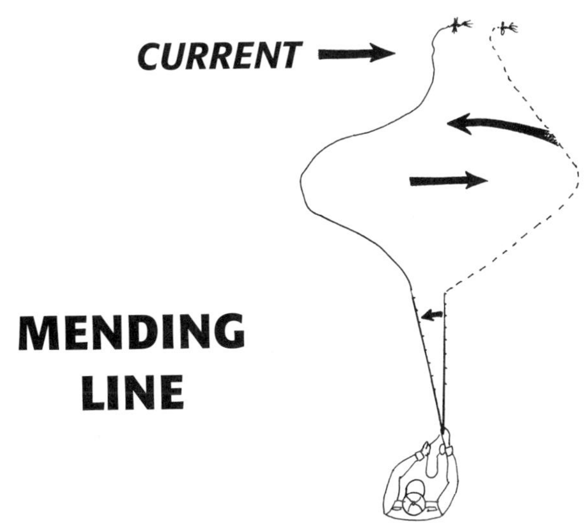

Mending line is a technique used to prevent the current from moving the line faster than the fly is moving, creating drag which will cause trout to reject a fly. Line is mended by rolling the mid-section of the line upstream with the rod tip as shown. The mend may disturb the drift but only momentarily. Until the current removes the mend, the fly will drift naturally.

mer when streams are low, trout tend to set up in the tail of the pools, at the edge of the outfall, where they are in position to intercept any terrestrial that drifts by. Out in the open and in the low, clear water, they are easily spooked and quick to run for cover. But on a given day, if the fish are in the tail of one pool, that's where they are likely to be in other pools, as well.

At another time, say when the water is cold, the same trout may be up in the pool, lying in deep water, sheltered from the current in back of a submerged rock in the stream channel. Chances are trout will be found in similar locations in other pools in that same reach of stream.

7 PUTTING IT ALL TOGETHER

While presentation is critical to catching trout on a fly, consistent success in doing so requires the integration of a variety of information. Sites trout are most likely to occupy at the moment, the best positions from which to cast to those sites and the approach to those positions which are least likely to alarm the fish all can be identified by reading the water.

By integrating existing weather conditions; the depth, temperature and clarity of the water; seasonal insect emergence patterns and feeding activities of trout, presentation of the fly can be fine tuned and chances of success improved.

The following trout stream scenarios portray four different real-life stream problems to illustrate the way fly fishermen integrate what they learn from reading the water with weather and stream conditions, insect emergence patterns and trout behavior in selecting the fly to use and how best to present it. These scenarios and the problems they present to the fishermen are based on actual experiences as are the accompanying solutions to each specific problem situation.

Following these four examples are some additional scenarios depicting other problem situations for the fly fisherman. These are provided to test your understanding of integrating what you read in the water with other information to help you locate and approach trout and to select and present a fly in such a way that they will mistake it for the real thing.

Situation #1

Photo Scenario #1 – stream pool

Situation information:

Weather conditions: air temp. 85°F., bright sun, light breeze.

Water temperature: 65°F

Water depth: 1 ft. at head of pool, 3 ft. in center of pool, and 10 inches at lip.

Water conditions: low, clear, shaded by trees

Time of year: mid-July

Time of day: early afternoon

Miscellaneous: no flies seen emerging, occasional surface activity.

Solution #1

Drawing of Scenario #1 – stream pool

Solution information:

Probable location of trout: stations A, B, C, D, E, F, G.

Approach: from tail of pool; move slowly, keep low profile to avoid scaring trout which may be at stations A, B & C.

Fly Selection: based on time of year, absence of emerging aquatic insects, surface activity only occasionally, and stream-side forest habitat, terrestrial patterns (ants, beetles) are the appropriate choice. Alternate small nymphs imitating either free-living caddis larva (muskrat nymph) or mayfly nymph (Hare's ear).

Presentation: to avoid casting over (lining) any probable lie before the fly has been presented to it, present the fly to the probable lies in the following order: C, D, B, A, F, G, E.

Situation #2

Photo Scenario #2 – spring fed meadow stream

Situation Information:

Weather conditions: air temperature 75°F, sky clear, sunny.

Water temperature: 58°F

Water depth: 1 - 2 ft.

Water conditions: clear, slight current.

Time of year: early fall

Time of day: mid-morning

Miscellaneous information: no flies emerging, no surface activity, variable currents among and between grass beds.

Solution #2

Drawing of Scenario #2 – spring fed meadow stream

Solution information:

Probable location of trout: Stations A, B, C, D, E, F, G.

Approach: upstream, moving very slowly to avoid sending shock waves ahead which would

frighten trout; casting from instream risks alarming fish but drag caused by grass beds and cross currents makes presentation from the stream bank difficult.

Fly selection: In the absence of any surface activity, imitations of cress bugs and scuds which are abundant the year around in most spring creeks and small mayfly nymph imitations are appropriate choices in this situation. Later in the day grasshoppers, crickets and Japanese beetles are present and active, and depending on the success achieved with nymphs, imitations of these terrestrials might be an effective option.

Presentation: To avoid lining any of the probable lies, present the fly in the following sequence: D, A, B, C, G, F, E. Given the clear water and sluggish current, a fine (5X - 6X), limp tippet to create slack and mending line will aid in managing drag.

Situation #3

Photo Scenario #3 – stream riffle

Situation information:

Weather conditions: air temperature 73°F, sky clear, calm.

Water temperature: 60°F

Water depth: shallow but variable, ½ to 1½ ft.

Water conditions: clear, moderate current, instream cover plentiful.

Time of year: early to mid-spring

Time of day: early afternoon

Miscellaneous information: Emerging mayflies (March Browns) are drifting with the current short distances before leaving the water; flies are of moderate size, brownish-tan in color, with prominent up-right wings, saillike in appearance. Surface disturbances include bulges and head-up rises.

Solution #3

Drawing of Scenario #3 – stream riffle

Solution information:

Probable location of trout: head-up rises are

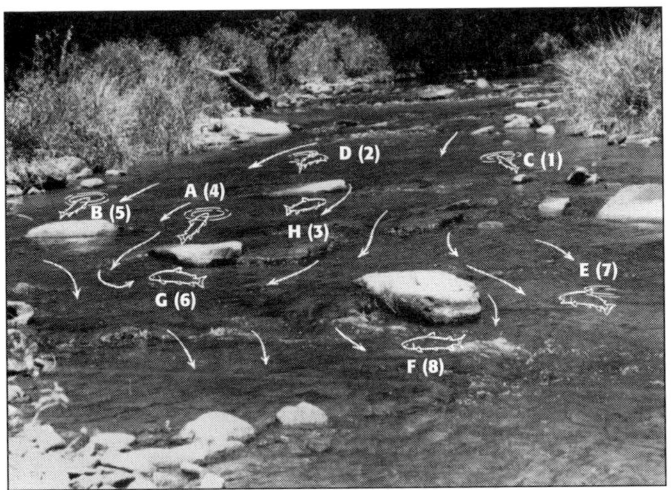

seen at A, B, and C; bulges are seen at stations D and E. Other lies here may also be occupied.

Approach: work upstream with dry flies or nymphs, move slowly and systematically to cover probable lies as well as active fish; or work downstream from head of riffle with wet flies or nymphs.

Fly Selection: if unfamiliar with the emerging mayfly, select a dry fly which matches it as close as possible in size and color; for nymph and wet fly pick a general mayfly nymph pattern or a wet fly of similar body size and color (brownish-tan).

Presentation (Upstream lies are indicated by letters. Downstream lies are indicated by numbers): Cast upstream with dry fly and nymph or downstream with wet fly or nymph. To avoid lining trout in other probable lies cast dry fly or nymph to upstream stations in the following order: F, G, B, A, H, E, C, D.

From the right margin of the stream, cast downstream and across with wet fly or nymph presenting the fly to the active trout and other probable lies in the following order: 1, 2, 3, 4, 5, 6, 7, 8.

☐ = your position

X

Exercise #1 (answers on page 82)

Photo scenario - mossy creek, meadow spring run

Situation information:

Weather conditions: air temperature 78°F, sky clear, sunny

Water temperature: 56°F

Water depth: variable, 1-3 ft. in most places

Water conditions: slightly milky, light current, rooted vegetation in channel

Time of year: early fall

Time of day: afternoon

Miscellaneous: limestone meadow stream, undercut banks, no fly hatch occurring

Write answers here:

approach: ____________________________________

____

____

fly selection ____________________________________

probable lies (indicated by letters) ________________

____

casting position & presentation sequence ________

____

Exercise #2 (answers on page 83)

Photo scenario - stream run

Situation information:

Weather conditions: air temperature 84°F, mixed clouds and sunny

Water temperature: 65°F

Water depth: variable, 10″ to 2 ft. in run, up to 5 ft. in pools

Water conditions: normal level, clear, moderate to fast current, large rocks and rubble in channel

Time of year: late spring/early summer

Time of day: morning

Miscellaneous: few caddisflies (dark color) are depositing eggs, occasional surface action by trout

Write answers here:

approach: ______________________________

____

fly selection ______________________________

probable lies (indicated by letters) ____________

casting position & presentation sequence ________

____

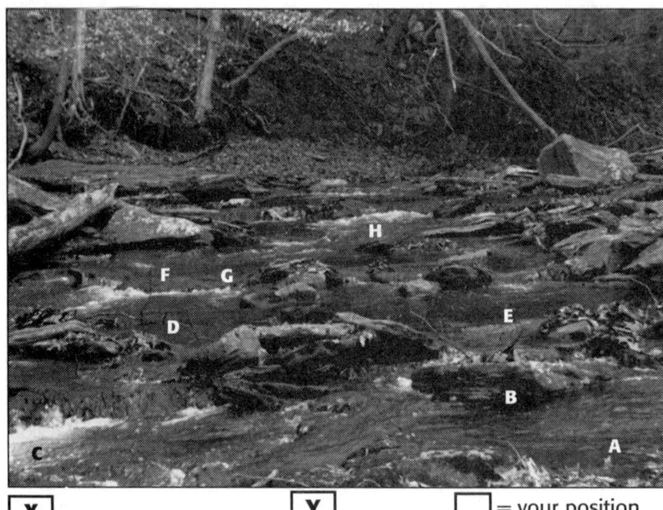

Exercise #3 (answers on page 84)

Photo scenario – pocket water

Situation information:

Weather conditions: air temperature 73°F, overcast, calm

Water temperature: 64°F

Water depth: variable, 6"- 24"

Water conditions: slight tinge of green, current variable, moderate to fast

Time of year: spring

Time of day: early afternoon

Miscellaneous: pocket water, small brown flies (maybe mayflies) hatching, surface feeding.

Write answers here:

approach: ________________________________

____

____

fly selection ________________________________

probable lies (indicated by letters) ____________

____

casting position & presentation sequence ________

____

Exercise #4 (answers on page 85)

Photo scenario — long, wide riffle

Situation information:

Weather conditions: air temperature 83°F, cloudy, light breeze

Water temperature: 60°F

Water depth: variable, 12″ to 18″

Water conditions: shaded, faint color, moderate current, rock and gravel bottom.

Time of year: late spring, early summer

Time of day: morning

Miscellaneous: no surface activity, no flies hatching, freestone stream with a variety of resident mayflies and caddisflies.

Write answers here:

approach: ______________________________

____

fly selection ______________________________

probable lies (indicated by letters) ______________

____

casting position & presentation sequence __________

____

□ = your position

Answers to Exercise #1 on page 78

Solution information:

Approach: from downstream position (for fishing terrestrial or nymph)

Fly selection: terrestrial (grasshopper, cricket)

Probable lies: B, C, D, E, G.

Presentation sequence & casting position: From casting position X–C, B, D, E; Move up to casting position Y–G.

Notes:

____

____

____

____

____

____

____

Answers to Exercise #2 on page 79

Solution information:

Approach: from downstream position for dry flies or nymphs; (alternate option) from upstream position for wet fly or streamer

Fly selection: dry fly - dark caddis imitation (dark elk hair caddis) matching size of egg laying insects; other options, caddis nymph imitation, or dark wet fly pattern.

Probable lies: B, C, D, E, G

Presentation sequence & casting position: (Dry fly or Nymph) from casting position X–B, C, D, E; move up to casting position Y–G. (Wet Fly) from casting position Y–G, E, D, C, B.

Notes:

Answers to Exercise #3 on page 80

Solution information:

Approach: from downstream positions

Fly selection: dry fly to match size and color of emerging insects

Probable lies: B, D, E, F

Presentation sequence and casting position: From casting position Y—B, E; Move to casting position X—D, F.

Notes:

Answers to Exercise #4 on page 81

Solution information:

Approach: from downstream with dry flies and nymphs; from upstream with wet fly selection

Fly selection: experiment with small to medium size, light colored mayfly and tan colored caddisly imitations; small to medium size nymphs and (from upstream position) wet fly patterns

Probable lies: A, C, D, E, F

Presentation sequence and casting position: From downstream position Y—A, C; Move to casting position X—F, D; Move to casting position Z—E. From upstream position V—D, C, A, F; Move to position W—E.

Notes:

8

DIFFERENT TROUT AND CHAR

Trout and char are important game and food fish. Primarily thought of as fresh-water fish, many of their number will spend some time in the sea. But they all will spawn in fresh water.

Most of your fishing experiences will revolve around rainbow trout and brown trout, with the brook trout a distant third in most parts. Brookies, as most fly fishermen refer to them, demand cleaner, cooler waters than the other two.

It's always a good idea to have a working knowledge of your quarry. The following pages should introduce you to the more popular members of the family Salmonidae and their allies.

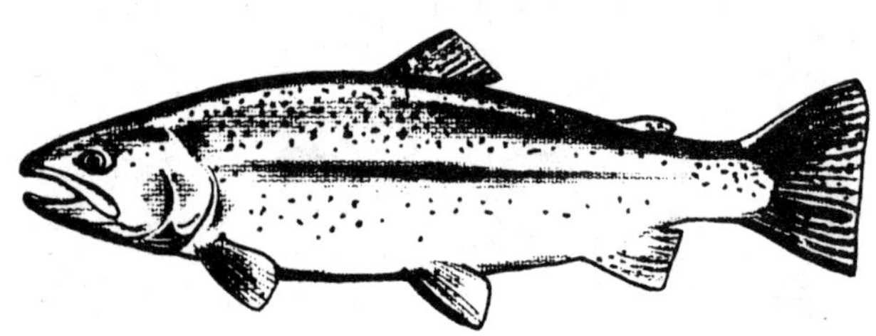

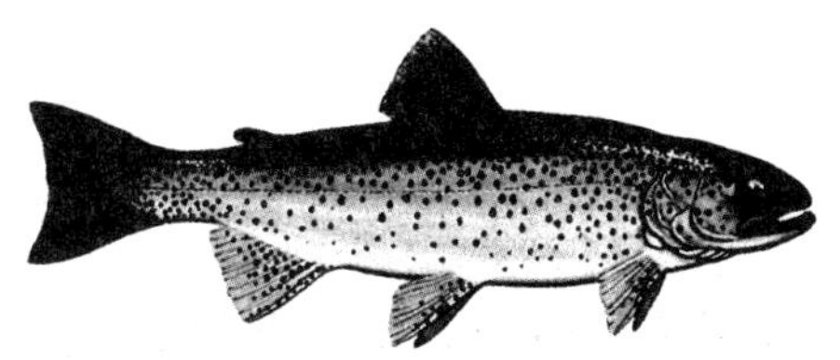

RAINBOW TROUT

(Oncorhynchus mykiss)
(formerly Salmo gairdneri)

This colorful and popular game fish is native to North America. Its original range extended from the highlands of northern Mexico to southern Alaska and the Aleutian Islands. Highly adaptable to hatchery environments, it has since been widely distributed in North America and has been exported to New Zealand, Australia, Tasmania, South Africa, Japan, Europe, Hawaii, and South America.

The species includes non-migratory races as well as sea and lake dwelling migratory races popularly known as steelhead. Rainbows vary greatly in color depending on age and habitat. Lake and ocean dwelling races are blue or green on the back, bright silver on the flanks and white on the belly. Stream dwelling rainbows are heavily spotted on the flanks, back, upper fins and tail. Mature fish develop a characteristic red lateral band and red cheeks. Ocean and lake dwelling races which migrate into streams to spawn take on the coloration of the mature stream dwellers soon after they enter the spawning streams.

Rainbows tolerate temperatures between 32°F and 89°F but 70°F is their preferred temperature level. They also tolerate a relatively wide range of pH. Rainbows may live for 7 to 11 years depending on the race and habitat. Inland rainbows typically spawn from January through June but through selection hatchery strains have been developed that will spawn at all months of the year.

Rainbows eat a varied diet including aquatic and terrestrial insects, fish eggs, small fish, annelids, sow bugs, and crayfish. In a stream environment they will inhabit pools, riffles, and undercut banks, where water conditions are suitable and food and cover are available.

BROWN TROUT

(Salmo trutta)

Brown trout are native to Europe from the Mediterranean to the Black Sea. A strain of brown trout was introduced to United States from Germany in 1883 and first stocked in the Pere Marquette River in northern Michigan. Another strain was imported later from Loch Leven in Scotland. As happened to the rainbow, the brown trout is now well distributed in North America with reproducing populations, including some sea run populations, in streams and lakes in the U.S. and Canada. Brown trout have also been introduced into New Zealand, South America, and parts of Asia and Africa.

The word “streamline” is used to describe the shape of the brown trout body. Stream dwelling brown trout are a golden brown with large black or brown spots on the sides of the body and a scattering of red spots in the lateral band. The spots are surrounded by a pale halo. The dorsal and adipose fins of older trout frequently are rimmed with orange or scarlet. The bellies of older trout from large stream systems tend to be yellow while the bellies of browns from smaller streams are more often creamy-white.

Although there are exceptions, brown trout generally are slightly less tolerant of warm water than are rainbows. The preferred temperature range extends from 54°F to 63°F. Browns also are able to tolerate a wide range of pH, with 6.8 to 7.8 being optimal. The more alkaline waters tend to produce larger fish. Depending on food and habitat, brown trout may live for 10 or 12 years. They spawn in late autumn or early winter when the water temperature drops to below 50°F.

Aquatic and terrestrial insects make up a large part of the diet of younger brown trout which forage to a large extent on the surface. Older, larger browns are notoriously cautious and quick to seek shelter and reluctant to leave it, feeding often at night. The large browns feed heavily on bait fish and crayfish.

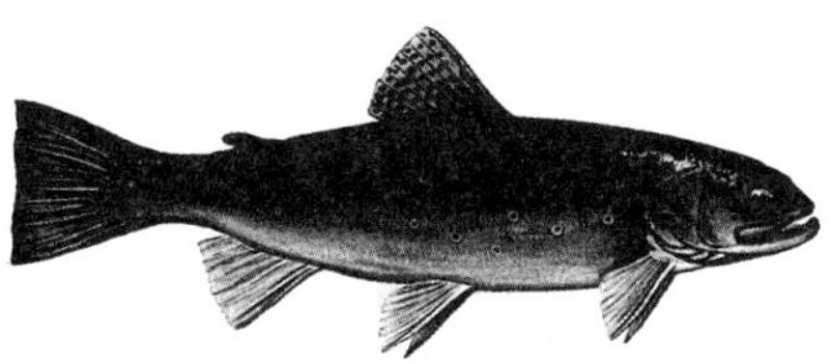

BROOK TROUT

(Salvelinus fontinalis)

The brook trout is the only true native trout in eastern North America. Its original range extended from the uplands of Georgia north to the Arctic Circle. Brookies have since been introduced into the remainder of the U.S. and Canada and into South America and Europe. Dark, wavy lines of pigmentation, called "vermiculations," on the brookie's back serve as camouflage. The sides of the body, which vary from grayish-green to a pale gray, are decorated with greenish-yellow spots and a scattering of small red dots, each surrounded by a pale blue halo. The belly of the fish is white, the leading edge of the lower fins are white.

Brook trout require clean, cold water. Brookies do not do well in water that exceeds 68°F; they prefer temperatures between 57°F and 62°F. They are able to tolerate a relatively wide range of pH, from 4.0 to 9.8, but do not fare as well at either extreme. A few sea-run populations of brook trout are known to exist in the more northern reaches of the range.

The typical stream brookie measures between 8 and 10 inches but some northern lakes and river systems in Canada produce brook trout weighing five pounds or more. Spawning occurs in the fall, starting in September in the more northern portions of the range but as late as December in the southern reaches. The bodies of male brookies turn vivid red or orange during spawning season.

In recent years, brookies have been transplanted all over the United States. Normally found at upper elevations, they have done quite well. This is especially true in the western states where a population of freshwater shrimp is available for feeding purposes. In fact, in some western areas the brook trout has become a problem because of overpopulation.

Aquatic insects, annelids, leeches and small fish such as sculpins and darters make up the bulk of the brook trout diet. Brook trout seldom live more than four years in the wild.

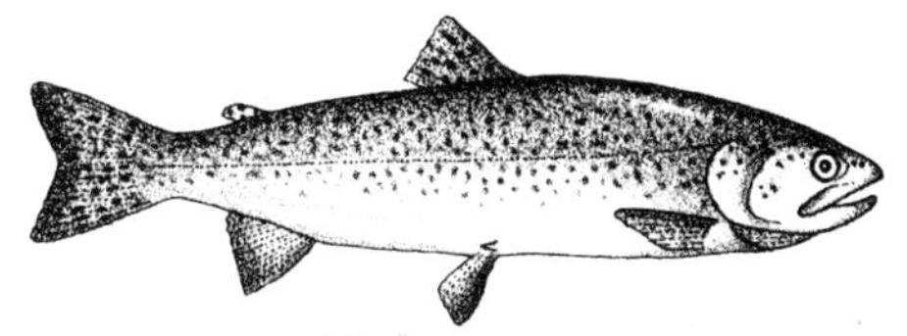

CUTTHROAT TROUT

(Salmo clarki)

The "cutthroat" is a native of the western states. It's found along the coast from Alaska to Northern California and inland from the Rocky Mountains to the Pacific Ocean. Salmo clarki includes many subspecies, some of which are sea-run populations. The body color varies considerably but all cutthroats have a narrow crimson band or slash along the lower jaw which is the origin of the name "cutthroat." Most individuals have spots on their sides, varying from sparse and dark to numerous and pale. The color of the back varies from green to greenish-yellow. Cutthroats hybridize readily with rainbows but the offspring of such matings retain the characteristic "cut" line on the lower jaw.

While found in rivers, lakes and salt water throughout its range, the cutthroat does not compete well with other fish and does not fare well in the face of heavy fishing pressure.

Cutthroats spawn from winter through spring; female cuts are said to spawn every two years instead of every year. The inland populations spawn in April and May while the coastal strains spawn in February and March. The life span for cutthroats is around 6 to 9 years.

Major items of the cutthroat's diet in fresh water are freshwater shrimp and aquatic insects including damselflies, midges, mayflies and caddisflies. The ocean diet of sea-run fish includes sand lances, shrimp and small fish. Mature sea dwelling cuts will weigh from 4 to 17 pounds. Freshwater seldom exceed 5 pounds.

9

SAFETY & ETIQUETTE

Safety experts claim there is no such thing as an accident. Injuries happen for a reason, so they can be avoided. The most common injuries associated with trout fishing result from falling, exposure to environmental forces or encounters with dangerous wildlife.

Whether in the stream or on the bank, the risk of falling is lessened by watching where you step and by moving slowly. Wearing polaroid sunglasses, which cut glare and allow you to see the stream bottom, and using a wading staff reduce the likelihood of a fall.

Also, the chance of slipping and falling in the stream can be greatly reduced by the addition of felt, metal cleats or both to the soles of wading shoes or boots.

If you are just beginning to fly fish, stay away from deep, fast flowing streams. Fast moving water can be difficult and even dangerous to wade; the faster the stream, the deeper the water and the more uneven the bottom, the more likely it is the current will sweep you off your feet. By the time you realize you're in trouble, it may be too late to return to shore.

When wading a stream, take slow, shuffling steps, moving the foot which is upstream first. Wear a wader belt with chest high waders to keep out water in case you fall. And if you do fall, try to direct your legs and feet downstream and use your arms to steer yourself towards shore.

Wear clothing appropriate for the season. Protect any exposed skin from the sun with sunblock. Polaroid glasses and a fishing cap or hat will protect your eyes and your head from a misdirected fly.

There are a couple of ways to remove a fly should it become embedded in your skin. Unless it is close to an eye, a small fly, especially a barbless one, can be removed in the field and the wound treated with antiseptic. Larger hooks which have penetrated beyond the barb are better removed in an emergency room.

If a thunderstorm catches you on the stream, seek shelter away from tall trees. Your graphite fly rod is a lightning attractor, too, so set it aside until the storm passes.

As a safety precaution, let someone know where you are going and when you plan to return before you venture out. If you intend to fish a new location, inquire about the presence of poisonous snakes or other dangerous wildlife.

Stream etiquette is nothing more than courteous behavior towards other anglers, respect for the rights of landowners and concern for the well being of the stream and its fish. You are expected to treat others as you would have them treat you.

If you come upon another angler, whether he's fishing or resting a spot, get out of the stream and walk around him, staying far enough away from the bank to avoid frightening his fish. If you are fishing downstream, yield the right of way to anglers who are fishing upstream. Leave the stream well in advance since any debris you dislodge may disturb the water downstream.

When you pass another angler, give him some room. Don't cut him off by fishing the next run or pool. Or if you see another angler moving towards a pool you want to fish, don't try to beat him to it or crowd him while he's fishing it. Wait until he moves on or go around him and come back to fish it later.

GLOSSARY

ACTION degree of bending of rod blank from tip to butt as it loads and unloads during casting stroke.

ATTRACTOR FLY a fly that lures fish by attraction rather than imitation.

AQUATIC INSECT insect which spends most of its juvenile life under water but emerges to reproduce.

BACKCAST that portion of the casting stroke in which the loop forms and unrolls to the rear.

BACKING strong, small diameter line used as an extension of fly line; also fills portion of reel spool not needed to store line which is not in use.

DOUBLE TAPER LINE a fly line with identical tapers at each end and a middle section of uniform diameter.

DRAG (fly) a condition in which a fly is moving faster than the current; with floating fly, drag produces a visible wake which causes trout to reject the fly.

DRAG (reel) the braking mechanism of a reel which prevents the reel spool from revolving freely.

DRIFT refers to the downstream travel of a fly being moved along only by the flow of the stream.

DRY FLY an artificial constructed to float on the water; it may be an attractor or designed to imitate an adult mayfly, caddisfly, stonefly or some other aquatic insect.

DUN mayfly which has emerged from water but is not yet sexually mature; will shed within 24 to 48 hours and become a spinner.

EMERGER an aquatic insect in the act of leaving the water to mate and complete its life cycle.

FERRULE the structure used to join and hold the rod tip butt together.

FLOATANT any of various water repelling substances applied to dry flies to help keep them afloat.

FORWARD CAST that part of the casting stroke in which the loop forms and unrolls forward.

HATCH refers to the periodic, usually annual, emergence of aquatic insects in preparation for mating.

LEADER less visible connector between fly line and fly; may be monofilament or braided, of various lengths and it may or may not be tapered.

LIMESTONE STREAM spring-fed, biologically rich stream rich in calcium carbonate, productive trout habitat.

LOADING the bending of the rod under the weight of the fly line.

MEMORY refers to the coiling which occurs when monofilament stored on a spool dries and assumes the shape of the spool.

MENDING LINE the act of laying a loop of line upstream to prevent current from taking line downstream faster than fly, causing drag.

NYMPH the larval stage of certain aquatic insects such as mayflies and stoneflies.

PATTERN directions for tying a particular fly, including the specific materials to be used.

PRESENTATION the act of casting a fly to trout or to a location where a trout might be holding.

POLAROIDS sunglasses with lenses which enable the wearer to see beneath the surface by eliminating glare.

SHOOTING LINE the act of releasing additional line immediately after the rod unloads forming the loop which pulls the additional line with it, increasing distance the cast covers.

SINGLE ACTION REEL fly reel in which the spool makes one complete revolution with each turn of the reel handle.

STRIPPING GUIDE the first one or two ring-like guides above the rod handle which aid in shooting line.

SPINNER a mayfly which has shed its skin for the final time and is ready to return to the water to lay eggs.

TERRESTRIAL a land-borne insect such as an ant, beetle, grasshopper or a cricket which may accidentally fall in the water.

TIPPET the limber tip section of the leader, usually between 12 and 18 inches long, which is tied to the fly.

TROUT'S WINDOW a circular area on the surface of the water which allows a trout to see objects on the surface and above it.

WEIGHT FORWARD LINE a fly line with tapered front end and a small-diameter line backing it; good for long casts.

WET FLY fly designed to simulate swimming and emerging aquatic insects; tied as imitators and attractors.

BASIC REFERENCES FOR BEGINNERS

Flick, Art. Art Flick's New Streamside Guide to Naturals and Their Imitations. Crown Publishers, Inc., 1969. Second printing. An excellent introduction to the classic mayfly hatches of the Northeast.

Hafle, Rick and Scott Roederer. An Angler's Guide to Aquatic Insects and Their Imitations For All North America. Johnson Books, 1995. Revised edition.

Hughes, Dave. Handbook of Hatches. Stackpole Books, 1987. A basic guide to identifying trout foods and selecting flies to match them.

Hughes, Dave. Reading the Water. Stackpole Books, 1988. A fly fisher's handbook for finding trout in all types of water.

Hughes, Dave. Tackle and Techniques For Taking Trout. Stackpole Books, 1990. Contains information about fly tackle selection and casting techniques.

Hughes, Dave. Tactics for Trout. Stackpole Books, 1990. This book covers tactics used to fish for trout with dry flies, wet flies, nymphs and streamers.

Hughes, Dave. Wet Flies. Stackpole Books, 1995. On tying and fishing subsurface flies, soft-hackles, winged and wingless wets and fuzzy nymphs.

Talleur, Richard W. The New Fly-Fishing for Trout. Winchester Press, 1987. An easy and enjoyable book written as a guide for beginners.